ESTATE PLANNING:

THE HEROES WAY FOR BABY BOOMERS!

SECOND EDITION:

THE ESTATE PLAN BEFORE AND AFTER 2010

By

Mark S. Cornwall, Esq.

ESTATE PLANNING:

THE HEROES WAY FOR BABY BOOMERS!

SECOND EDITION:

THE ESTATE PLAN BEFORE AND AFTER 2010

by
Mark S. Cornwall

All publishing information or other inquiries should be directed to Baby Boomer Publishing, 210 East Figueroa St., Santa Barbara, CA, 93101.

Visit our websites at:
BabyBoomerPublishing.com
TheHeroesWay.com
MarkCornwall.com

Dedicated to:

My loving wife D'Arcy
and my beautiful daughter Aurora,
without whom I would not care if I had an
estate plan, except to make certain
everything transfers to them tax free.

Author's Disclaimer

This book is not intended to be legal advice or create a lawyer/client relationship. It is for general information and educational purposes only, and specifically to help guide you into a vision of your legacy to take to a qualified attorney's office to assure its legality.

Every care has been taken to verify that the representations are correct and accurate, but the current state of the law in all states is constantly changing. Do not rely on the legal facts without first checking with a licensed attorney, particularly if you do not live in California, to better understand how your own state Laws affect you and the Federal Law.

No opinion herein is a "marketed opinion" and no information provided herein can be used to avoid tax penalties for which the taxpayer would otherwise be responsible. This book provides you with one attorney's perspective of estate planning, and is intended to be helpful in communicating those ideas to others.

TABLE OF CONTENTS

CHAPTER SIX

CHAPTER SEVEN

CHAPTER EIGHT

CHAPTER NINE

CHAPTER TEN

CHAPTER ELEVEN

CHAPTER SIXTEEN

CHAPTER SEVENTEEN

CHAPTER EIGHTEEN

CHAPTER NINETEEN

CHAPTER TWENTY

CHAPTER TWENTY-ONE

CHAPTER TWENTY-TWO

CHAPTER TWENTY-THREE

CHAPTER TWENTY-FOUR

CHAPTER TWENTY-FIVE

CHAPTER TWENTY-SIX

INTRODUCTION

This book is one of a kind because it answers the question, "How do you help people stare their mortality in the face and enjoy it, as they develop a plan to distribute everything they own after their death?"

One way is to convince them if they do not do something about it, their heirs are going to lose 55% of everything you or you and your spouse have worked for your entire life. If you plan on living longer than the year 2010 and your estate is valued over $1 million, it is scheduled by law that everything over that amount be taxed at a rate of 55% -- including savings, IRAs, securities, pensions, cars, boats, jewelry, art work, coin collections, gun collections, tapestries, pool tables and pools. It is going to the government straight past your descendants or charities, and right out of your children's pockets.

Doing nothing is not the hero's way of handling this. Leaving it all to your wife (it is always assumed the husband goes first because statistics prove it in the majority) is not the hero's way either because it will only double the value of her estate. As a result your children will pay twice the taxes when she dies then if you had taken a few simple steps in estate planning.

The first step is to read this book and determine how the system works so you can take full advantage of the "Credit Shelter Trusts" the government has given you to help your children avoid losing your estate to taxes.

This book was written for one reason only. It is intended to motivate you to get your estate plan done now - not later. This is the purpose of the book and it does so with the help of the most efficacious, least expensive, and understandable explanations, using flow charts that make it simple to follow the most up to date law. It also defines the methods of creating and finishing your Revocable Trust. The idea is to move you into action with the least possible effort. The first thing is to learn the talk so you can walk the walk.

What encourages you to do so is having a Master Plan by a hero who, by virtue of his being, makes the task of estate planning worth emulating; a hero, like the father of our country George Washington. He wrote more than 20,000 letters during his life and he still had time to write his 29 page Will explicitly naming everything he owned and everybody who was to receive each part of it. There is no better example than Washington to prove no person is too busy or preoccupied not to take care of business at home. He also added with each bequest in his Will his comments as to the gift's meaning and his suggestions as to how and when it should be used.

More importantly, Washington's Last Will and Testament included emancipating his 600 slaves; the first president to do so, and it was not done again by the next eight presidents who were all slave owners. It was 64 years before others followed suit, including the great Thomas Jefferson who died 27 years after Washington. Jefferson did not emancipate his slaves, using business hardship as his excuse. So who was the greatest American visionary of all time?

It is Washington's tested values and leadership abilities that will help you to finally get this much needed document called a Revocable Trust prepared. Of course, times have changed dramatically since Washington was alive. Fortunately for him there was no estate tax when he died. There were no volumes upon volumes of Internal Revenue Codes and Regulations to follow.

Built within the IRS Code and Regulations system are also certain tax exemptions and deductions. If you know what they are and are not afraid to learn about them, you can save your estate thousands upon thousands, if not millions of dollars, and substantial stress and chaos for your family, friends and special causes.

The reason I am writing this second edition (my first edition was published in 2006) is because the first edition had sufficient information about the estate planning lexicon, and practical scenarios, but it lacked a compelling argument to motivate most people to do more than just talk about it.

I have a very good friend who lives up the coast, and although I had given him another copy of the previous book with a questionnaire in the back, he has twice called me, six months apart, and asked me to send him a copy of the questionnaire because he really wanted to start putting his new Revocable Trust together.

His last one, the $650 "boilerplate" production, was written years ago when he was still married to his second wife. He had recently remarried, and in my opinion his Revocable Trust was nothing but trouble – particularly because he had four children by two previous marriages, four grandchildren since then, along with amassing substantially more assets.

Six months has again passed and he still has done nothing to start his new Revocable Trust. Although we speak on a regular basis, he just does not want to talk about it.

It made me wonder, how many other Baby Boomers are there like this in America, and more challenging was how to get them to move forward on the project? Since it is a subject no one wants to talk about due to the grizzly mix of death and having to split property amongst your children, or brothers and sisters and cousins, etc., (and some are more deserving then others), it makes it tough and emotional.

I thought, if only there was a hero who led by example and could be respected by everyone as a person whose virtues they would want to emulate, then this might be the catalyst that brings the whole mix of estate planning into a finished product. But where do you find a hero in estate planning?

It all became clear to me after taking a trip to Valley Forge and Mt. Vernon. The rest of the story is revealed in the book. I hope it works for you as it did for me.

ESTATE PLANNING:

THE HEROES WAY FOR BABY BOOMERS!

SECOND EDITION: THE ESTATE PLAN BEFORE AND AFTER 2010

CHAPTER ONE

What This Country Needs is a *HERO*

Assuming you know absolutely nothing about estate planning, you at least know that if you plan on doing it, you must know your assets. Assets consist of everything you own, paid for or not. They are characterized as either separate, community, or quasi-community property with your wife or husband. Obviously, this does not apply to single individuals.

One thing that was missing in the first edition of *"Everything a Baby Boomer Should Know..."* published in 2006, was that the book had no major character who defied all odds and led others into action by example of their own virtue. Every good book needs a hero...and we are talking about a major superhero! But where would you find a hero for estate planning in this or any other age?

The only names presently seen or heard on the news these days regarding estate planning are those anti-heroes of large corporations whose heroism is reduced to estate tax **evasion** planning while they indignantly insist they deserve the riches they have stolen. They do this while either sitting in prison waiting for news on their appeal to have their conviction overturned, or have so much money they can keep the wheels of justice spinning until they die.

Let's examine two of America's worst fraudulent financial anti-heroes: the two Enron Fat Cats. First, Kenneth Lay, 64 years old, who was allowed to remain out of prison on bail after being convicted to a life sentence in May of 2006. He died of a heart attack in July of 2006 in Colorado making it impossible to recover the millions of dollars he stole from investors. Yes, he had an iron clad estate plan.

Then there is his indignant successor Jeffrey Skilling, who at 52 years old, was convicted on many counts of "classic securities fraud" and sentenced to 24 years in prison. He is at a Minnesota federal prison where he has been waiting for his appeal to be heard before a panel of three federal judges. Skilling blamed his conviction on the spiteful temperament of the Houston venue where his trial was heard. (Can you wonder why?) He is hopeful his case will be reversed on appeal, "after everyone calms down."

That day came on April 3, 2008, when Skilling's attorney argued before a panel of judges in New Orleans that his conviction should be thrown out because Skilling always provided "honest services" to Enron as its chief executive. The argument is that Skilling is not guilty because his loyal services benefited Enron, even if his services were fraudulent. He claims he never deprived Enron of his "loyal, honest attempts to make a profit."

It will be months before the court returns its opinion, but it is rather obvious what the investors, employees and retirees who were the victims of Skilling's fraudulent services must be thinking. They are no doubt asking, "Who the hell is Enron if not us?" Nevertheless, chief executives have won appeals using this argument before. They served the company. How could things be more turned upside down than that?

So what about a real hero from a different time in the history of our country? Have you ever thought just before doing something about your estate plan of excuses such as: not now, later, or, I have too much on my plate, or, I don't plan on dying today, or, it's too complicated, I don't want to talk to my spouse about this, I want to go water skiing, it's going to cost too much, I'll just have my attorney do it, my estate's not big enough, I'm too young, I'll do it after my last kid graduates, I sent away for the CD forms, I'll figure them out because the salesperson said it would be easy for everyone, ...and on and on the excuses pass you by, and then you die.

Now think about the man in America's history known for being the General of the Continental Army, who won the War of Independence, then became our first President. He was so respected by everyone that our nation's capital is named after him. After his precedent setting two term presidency he retired to design and manage the largest distillery and one of the largest farms in Virginia called Mt. Vernon.

Most impressively, with over 600 slaves living on the farm, he set them free upon his wife's death two years after his own. That was 27 years before the death of Thomas Jefferson who was not willing to set his slaves free upon his death, nor did the next eight presidents after Washington, who owned slaves to make their living. Such was the leadership, the vision and the example set by the father of our country – George Washington.

George Washington is our estate planning hero because despite all that was on his democratic plate, he also personally kept track of everything he owned in his own script, (and he had a lot of it, particularly land). He made certain that upon his death each asset was distributed to the person to whom he intended to bequeath it, along with his comments on the expectation of its use.

By today's law, if those lands are not funded into a Revocable Trust, you must go through each state's probate where the land is located in order to execute the exchange of property. I repeat, you have to go to the state where their property is located and probate it in order to own it. Think of the time and expense.

Of course there was no estate tax at the time of Washington's death in 1799, but he is a gleaming example of the organizational skills necessary to make sure all his assets were accounted for in his personal life. Most of his life was given to public service, including the seven winters he spent at Valley Forge, the most famous being the winter of 1777-78. This was the Winter Washington held the Continental Army together through rampant disease, lack of equipment, and loss of battles. Martha Washington joined her husband on many occasions, as did other wives. During those winters of war, Martha did her share of attending to duties. Not everyone endured those miseries as they came close to defeat, yet, throughout those perils of war Washington never left his men.

All of the information provided above can be easily verified by a trip to Mount Vernon, Virginia, just 16 miles outside Washington D.C. But what you can also purchase at Mt. Vernon is the book containing The Last Will and Testament of George Washington, all 29 pages of it. It also contains the Last Will and Testament of Martha Washington. The book is edited by John C. Fitzpatrick and published by the Mount Vernon Ladies' Association of the Union, by Foley and Lardner in 2003.

The "Schedule of Property" making up the assets in the Will is written entirely in George Washington's own hand (which is not in the book) and was drawn up by him without any legal aid of any kind, although he held honorary law degrees from five of the most prestigious universities in the young nation. However, in defense of the legal profession, he did appoint his nephew, Bushrod Washington, an associate justice to the Supreme Court, as one of the executors of the Will.

It can neither go unrecognized nor be underestimated how far ahead of his time George Washington was. As pointed out by former Justice of the Supreme Court, Justice Lewis F. Powell, Jr., on the issue of slavery, Washington's vision for the future of America as of 1799 was far beyond the sight of his peers. He was no ordinary man.

Justice Powell writes: "Especially after the Revolution, Washington had become increasingly troubled by the 'peculiar institution'. He favored abolition of slavery by gradual measures, and wrote privately: "Not only do I pray for it, on the score of human dignity, I can clearly foresee that nothing but rooting out of slavery can perpetuate the existence of the Union."

What is important about the times is that Washington knew he could not abolish slavery by himself, as it was a fact that all the land owning gentry amongst his peers were slave owners. But he addresses the emancipation of slavery at length in his Will where his moral duty compelled him to use his Last Will and Testament as a torch on the subject leaving no doubt of his sentiment for change by emancipating his slaves.

Compare this to the fact that Thomas Jefferson's excuse for not freeing his slaves upon his death 27 years later was due to his financial hardship, the same excuse used by the South before the Civil War. When you add to this the fact that none of the next eight presidents after Washington emancipated their slaves, this is where you begin to understand what a hero is. It's a man of great vision and moral integrity who is not afraid to lead the way to a better life for everyone, and that is what you want to be, and can be, after reading this book, starting with an estate plan because that is what most affects your family's well being after you are gone.

The way it will turn out for all Baby Boomers is the only person who is not going to die a hero's death is the man or woman who does not have an estate plan, and who dies intestate. It is not a heroic way to leave your heirs. The person who leaves their heirs behind to face the financial and stressful burden of going to court to figure out who gets what is no hero.

What George Washington's Will exemplifies is that you can do with your property whatever you want, be it grand, or just a closure, or the last statement of your life. What follows in this "does not contain Everything" you should know about estate planning because nobody knows that much. To reach that height of acuity you need experts in law, accounting, transfer taxation, insurance, valuation, trust annuities and actuary tables, long term care, trustees, and much more depending on the size and scope of your estate.

This book gives you ideas and comparable scenarios for regular responsible Americans to use to help themselves formulate what is right for their family, and helps explain what to do to distribute their legacy to the ones they love. All the information necessary is in this book, or at least enough to get you started and finished. How far you want to go is up to you.

CHAPTER TWO

This Time You Will Succeed

Do the names Jimi Hendrix, Janis Joplin, or Jim Morrison conjure up any memories of excitement or good times in the sixties and seventies? How about bad times? If so, this book is for you. They didn't live long enough to worry about their estate plan, but you did. Congratulations!

Now, what are you going to do about it? I have poster art in my office of Jimi Hendrix (worth $7,500), Janis Joplin and Jim Morrison (worth $750 each), but what am I going to do with it when I am dead? Will anybody care, or will they all fight over the Hendrix poster?

Not all estate plans are the same, and most likely no one has taught you anything about death and inheritance. You may still believe what you see on TV, including the drama of the "reading of the Will," where the family sits around the attorney's teak desk as he informs them of their inheritance. But in reality, there is no such law that demands that scenario, and it will not happen unless the executor or attorney purposely wants it to happen for some odd reason.

Besides their lack of knowing what to do, one of the reasons Baby Boomers, or any other couples, are so reluctant to do estate planning is that it's a depressing subject. It's not much fun thinking about being dead and leaving your loved ones behind, even though that is exactly what is going to happen to every one of us.

What is worse is thinking about those loved ones fighting over your property and family heirlooms after you are gone. But what seems to be even worse, or harder to do, is for a husband and wife to sit down and talk about the distribution of their property. At least that is what they think because they are thinking about it in the wrong way. I should know. I have been trying to get couples to do it since I wrote the first edition of this book two years ago. They read it and continue to do nothing, or it is still sitting on their desk.

In a marriage where the husband brought the house, the toys, the pension and other separate property into the marriage, while, by comparison, the wife had very little to contribute, a strange phenomena can occur during these discussions.

Please read this very carefully. An honest and open conversation with your wife or husband about who owns how much of the community property, and what is separate and what is not, can lead to arguments so bitter you might decide to

forget estate planning and let it all go to Hell. It is a fact that most schedules of property attached to a Revocable Trust which clarify what percentages are community and what part are separate, are not accurate (which is why you should not do it that way). The owner of the separate property usually condescends into allowing the other spouse a much larger portion than what is real because they do not want to fight over what the other spouse insists they own, even if they own none of it. They think that sharing property makes it community property, which is not correct.

Do not let that happen. Even if it seems you are going through a divorce rather than writing or planning your estate plan, understand there are rules that need to be followed. There is too much at stake, especially if you have children from a previous marriage, to do nothing about the ownership of your separate property because your children will gradually have it pulled out from under them and they will end up with next to nothing. This major issue is discussed at length at many CEB estate planning seminars, with emphasis on how to deal with it.

Compromise if you must. Be open minded and put yourself in their shoes. If you still cannot agree because one party feels emotionally that they own 50% of your separate property and they want 100%, and you cannot get beyond it, send them to another attorney to have the facts of life explained to them.

This is where attorneys can be very helpful in unraveling what is a huge miscommunication. Most people know nothing about estate planning, and when you start talking percentages of community property they do not understand what a "three way formula split" is. They need to understand that without a transmutation agreement, they cannot possibly own more than 25% of the community property if it was 100% your separate property when they came into the marriage.

Stay calm, take a deep breath, and work it out because you love them, and you would not leave them not provided for, and that is the fear they have. The surviving spouse wants to keep the same level of lifestyle they had before you died. This is why a Disclaimer Trust is not generally suggested as a good idea. It is because this fear of not having enough to last them their entire lives keeps them from disclaiming anything, and wanting to keep it all in their Survivor's Trust. This fear far outweighs any desire to avoid or defer taxes upon their own death, because then it will be at someone else's expense.

Fear Prohibits Us From Finishing

The reason for writing a second edition so soon after the first is not because the laws have changed, nor that they are going to change. The reason is because the first book failed to inspire couples into action. All the information was in the book, but there was no inspirational call to arms. Plenty of people loaded their guns, but none of them fired their guns all at once, "and floated into space," as Steppenwolf would have said. They preferred to remain frozen like a deer in the headlights. The excuses stretched from the ubiquitous "no time," to the inevitable, "I'll do that next week, or next year."

Therefore, this second book is taking on a different format, which actually makes it a different book. I am going to relieve your fears and lead you right down the primrose path with surefooted steps that will get you where you want to go. It is not going to be the shotgun format as before where information is scattered as defined across the chalkboard for you to pick and choose what you think is right for your family from a flowchart.

This time I am going to tell you what is right for you and if you don't like it that's great! At least it means you are beginning to know what you are talking about and that you are thinking about how *you* want to distribute your legacy in a better way. Then you can do the job the way you want. Just do it!

Admittedly, this second edition was much easier to write then the first. That is because I have come from being the struggling attorney attempting to put into layman's terms extremely complicated legal language such as "a three-way split with a nonmarital pecuniary formula clause" and become the writer who has seen the looks on people's faces when I mention that term. Those faces are just begging me to do it for them -- regardless of the outcome, even though, because of a lack of proper communication, it may not be what they wanted.

There is certainly nothing wrong with getting a little help, or a lot of it, and hopefully this book will be your best friend when it comes to issues of death, inheritance, and the distribution of your wealth, whether it is big or small. I am very dedicated in helping resolve the issues involved with blended and extended families, and there are estate planning tools, or in some cases legal "maneuvers," to meet your every need. We will get to them all; or at least enough to know when you want to stop.

Those with Probate Thrust Upon Them Need Help First

It is interesting to note that the people who were the most immediately appreciative of the first edition of "*Everything a Baby Boomer Should Know...*" were those people, young and old, who had probate problems thrust upon them. Either someone close to them just died, they inherited something blanketed in controversy, or someone they loved was on their deathbed. Rarely is the man or woman who is in good health and under 65 years old, ready to do estate planning quite yet – the exception being the very wealthy.

This experience has proven that the majority of people are not moved to action or to learning anything about the probate process and/or the distribution of inheritance through a Revocable Trust or by Last Will and Testament until it is almost too late. It is always someone who is never ready and who has waited until the last second. It is this second phenomenon I am fighting against because the people I see are the ones left behind after someone's death, and they are clueless about what to do next. That is why they are buying a book to help guide them through the crisis.

I am adamant that in most instances where there is a proper trustee, a Revocable Trust is by far preferred over a Will because it saves you or your loved ones the stress, cost, and delay of going to court. Court is where all the problems are. Judges are called upon daily to make decisions in cases concerning people's lives. It is their job to make decisions, and half of the time their mental process is not going to satisfy somebody.

In order to avoid any confusion in the terms Revocable Trust, or Living Trust, as used in this book, let me explain from the very beginning, there is no difference.

There is a popular trust package being sold these days at various seminars that promise all you need, regardless of your individual estate, is a Living Trust - kind of a cookie cutter claim that one-size-fits-all. *Caveat Emptor!* A Living Trust, standing alone, only works for the smallest estates where you have someone trustworthy enough to administer it in your absence. And it is still of no value if it is not funded, meaning, for example, your home is not changed into the name of the trust at the County Records Department.

My preference in calling it a Revocable Trust stems from the fact it is the legally preferred name, and because it serves as a reminder that it can be "revoked" and changed in any fashion you like while you are still alive. Revocable means you can change anything you want any time you want until the first spouse dies, or if there is no spouse, until you die.

The term "Living Trust" stems from the fact the correct legal name for the trust is a Revocable Inter-vivos Trust. "Inter-vivos" means "living." Because the trust only becomes effective if executed while you are alive, as contrasted with a Will which only becomes effective upon your death, comes the term "living." Secondly, I use the term Revocable Trust because I do not want it mixed up with what is being sold from a Living Trust paralegal mill for $650. They are not worth the money, and you will be convinced of that by the end of this book, or hopefully much sooner, those mill trusts will probably lead the administrator of the trust right back to an attorney's office and into probate court.

Another benefit of a Revocable Trust is that it can keep you or anyone you love from going through a conservatorship. This is where I get accused of being biased, but my personal experience, and the resulting feelings of seeing the judge appoint a professional conservator, (whom a client has never met before), along with the appointment by the conservator of his or her own health care entourage (who will regulate your every waking moment, decide what will or not be your desire, terminate your ability to make financial decisions and who you see, including family members, and use your money to drive you to the poor house), is the height of indignity for the Conservatee. This indignity extends to those who have cared for him or her for years, during and after a life of hard work. And, if you become disabled, a court procedure for a conservator is totally unavoidable.

Unfortunately when either the client took no action to avoid the conservatorship, or there simply is no person willing or able to assume the responsibility of running the estate while caring for the disabled, it becomes an absolute necessity.

There are several more reasons why you should get to work on your estate plan today and they will all be discussed, and analyzed in future chapters. This book is designed to tell you the exact way to create your plan. The specific steps will be laid out for you: one, two, three, etc., with a beginning, middle, and an end, after which, you will have mapped out a flowchart for yourself. This chart will show exactly where you want to go with your estate. After reading this book, you will have nothing left to do except put it into words.

And most importantly, you are going to allow attorneys to draft the trust for you because it is too complicated to do otherwise and they can be of great service to you. You will also make sure they have malpractice insurance in case they make a mistake in correctly consummating your request. In other words, you have someone responsible for drawing up your Revocable Trust incorrectly, besides yourself.

The overall plan is to get your fortune from your estate, regardless of the size, to the estate of your loved ones or charity without paying any estate taxes on the transfer. Somebody has worked very hard to lobby Congress for these estate planning tools, so it is up to you to be smart enough to use them where you can.

CHAPTER THREE

The Federal Estate Tax Law Applies to Every State

In this *Heroes* edition of "*Everything a Baby Boomer Should Know...*" I hope to answer the questions that arose from the first edition I wrote. During the last two years of listening to audiences and answering their questions, two main issues were identified:

1. Except for the couple who had nothing when they got married, the hardest thing for a husband and wife to do is sit down and talk about who owns how much of the property they refer to as "their" property. This is particularly true when one spouse comes into the marriage with lots of baggage, (some of it valuable and some not), and they must decide who gets the "power of appointment," which means who has the right to give it away. Unfortunately, this is the very first step to estate planning so it will be explored thoroughly after answering the next question.

2. The general public has a very vague idea of how the legal system works starting with both houses of Congress and the IRS, then down to our state legislators, and then out to our state court systems. People want black and white answers where there are only grey. That is why there are attorneys and it will behoove you to learn the tools of the trade, then use an attorney for liability purposes, just in case they make a mistake. Attorneys are also highly educated in legal matters and may have a better idea of accomplishing your general notions.

All of the estate principles and common law advice offered in this book are to educate and help you formulate a plan for distributing your wealth to your heirs, and not to the government.

Death tax in 2008 is 45% for any estate valued over $2 million. In 2009 it will be 45% on anything over $3.5 million. And in 2010 it is unlimited and there will be no death tax! But there is one huge obstacle in the way of ever getting the benefit of 2010 and that is the presidential election in 2008. What will happen in 2011 when the present estate tax law is put to rest under the present sunset provision? A detailed answer to this question is given in Chapter Ten.

As will be discussed under "The Marital Tax Exemption Tax," (also in Chapter Ten), there are numerous options the U.S. Legislature may take in recreating the estate tax laws. But as it stands today, with the Congress still refusing to vote on a new estate tax law and with the impending recession in 2008 calling for a drastic monetary bailout on all fronts, it does not look bright for the future of estate taxes or the lesser used gift tax, let alone the generation skipping tax.

The general consensus among estate planners is that the dollar amount for the federal marital tax exemption (at the death of the first spouse) or for any single estate, including the death of the surviving spouse, will revert to $1 million in 2011 with the increased percentage of tax being 55%, the highest tax in the nation, on everything over a $1 million valued estate. (That value includes everything from property, to tie clips.) Otherwise, things will remain the same.

So, as your estate continues to grow over the years, it is wise to learn these tools. It is a fact you will have to periodically update your estate plan as laws change, as well as with your personal and financial growth.

Therefore, learn the federally designed "estate planning tools" which are there to aid you in the distribution of wealth before you or your parents, or your children are gone. *After you are gone it is too late,* and that is unfortunate because each tool is designed to legally avoid and/or defer estate taxes. But, it must be implied while you are alive.

Think Big Picture

What makes it impossible to write a thorough analysis of all the twists and turns of estate planning as they apply to every state in the USA is that although a great number of people may live in community property states, their laws differ from each other as much as other states' laws that are considered not community property states. Each state has different and complex laws. Even community property states have vast differences.

For example, there are nine community property states, including California, Arizona, Idaho, Louisiana, Nevada, New Mexico, Texas, Washington and Wisconsin. (In Alaska you can choose whether or not you want a community property estate.)

In Idaho, Louisiana, Texas and Wisconsin if you own separate property, the income from that property is considered community property. That is not the law in California, unless you commingle it with community property funds with your spouse. If necessary, it can always be traced back to separate property in case of a divorce. But this same property is not traceable in the case of death.

Another example is that in most community property states, if you stop living with each other, your income becomes separate property, but not in all of the states.

So, in different states, there are going to be as many different ways of determining what is, and what is not separate or community property. State laws have the final say on how your property is going to be characterized before it is distributed according to federal law, also known as the Internal Revenue Code. State laws vary and are sometimes significant to other state's laws and can be easily misunderstood. Local law should always be consulted for applicability to your personal situation.

A specific example of confusing state laws is encapsulated in the concept of "quasi-community property." This type of property evolves when you lived in a non-community property state and acquired separate property that would have been community property had you been domiciled in a community property state such as Washington, California, or Arizona when you acquired the separate property. These states will treat it as community property and it will be characterized as such in your estate plan or divorce.

So regardless of the fact that the terms remain the same, they can be interchanged and treated much differently depending on what state you moved to when you wrote your Revocable

Trust, and under the laws of the state in which you come to rest.

Adding to this state law confusion, eighteen states have adopted the "Uniform Probate Code" (at least in part, and some with substantial changes). This Code is intended to allow all citizens to walk to the beat of the same drummer when entering probate court. Three community property states have adopted it, but 32 other states, such as California, have not adopted it at all. In fact, California has its own set of probate rules and procedures operating their superior courts the same as Texas and Florida have their own rules operating their higher courts.

What this means is that GRITs, QPRTs CRATs, CRUTs and other federal estate planning tools are all well defined and interpreted with some similarity in federal courts, but in all likelihood your case is never going to get there. All probate matters begin in state courts which for the most part are operating under different state laws and "Rules of Court." These rules of concept, analysis and implementation are created by state legislators.

Breaking it down further, every county in every State has "Rules of Court" pertaining particularly to how things will be handled by the courts n their particular county. There are 58 counties in California and many of them have rules quite different from the others. The differences may not be so substantial as to change the outcome of a case, but on every court bench there sits a different personality with his or her set of personal rules and bias.

In short, it is impossible to write any book or treatise on estate planning that provides black and white answers for every question arising from every county courthouse in this great nation. That is why this book is limited to the discussion of general overall provisions provided by the federal government for estate plans regardless of the individual state laws.

The important thing to remember is that you must always get the opinion from an attorney in your state before implementing the federal estate tools presented herein, or anyplace else. Not even Suze Orman would ever disagree with that advice, just read her disclaimers.

That is why this book is focused on Revocable Trusts rather than traditional Last Wills and Testaments. The Revocable Trust is your best bet for staying out of the court system.

A disclaimer, by the way, is what you find in the front of all books that hopefully keep the authors from being sued for what they have written. But for attorneys, a disclaimer has a much more onerous task that is spearheaded by IRS Circular 230.

This regulation is directed solely at attorneys and violation of it could lead to their disbarment. Some attorneys are so cautious they add a disclaimer to everything they put in print to assure the reader that no opinion in the attorney's missive is a "marketed opinion." It is necessary that the attorney's disclaimer include the magic words explaining "no information provided herein can be used to avoid tax penalties for which the taxpayer would otherwise be responsible."

So rest assured, you are being taught sound legal principles meant only to educate the general public of their legal rights.

Lastly, I have been an active member of the California State Bar for 26 years and cannot help but be affected by 26 years of legal eccentricities involving the active lives of California residents.

Adhering to the cardinal rule of writing, which is to write only what you know, I have tried to spice up the somewhat dull topic of estate planning with anecdotal stories from past experiences as well as new and unconventional laws initiated in California which may be of controversy in other States. This is done in the hope of getting you to think and do something about your estate plan. The more you know the less you will be afraid of it. And besides that, it has often been said, "As California goes, so goes the nation." And when you are talking about estate planning, it is a subject that goes on for years, so things can change. You must look into the future.

The purpose of this book is first to educate while trying to make the subject interesting, but mainly to spur you into action. Neither you nor anybody else wants you to die, let alone to die intestate (meaning no Will, no Revocable Trust). An estate plan is the best gift to leave your heirs, and they will thank you forever for having your affairs in order. You will die a hero.

CHAPTER FOUR

What's So Funny about Death and Inheritance?

The article written below was published in the *Santa Barbara Lawyer Magazine* in July of 2006.

This book's purpose is to answer questions that arise in the course of estate planning from beginning to end. The reason this article was published in the lawyer magazine is because every attorney knows every legal issue begins with a question, *ergo*, the judge's opening statement, "The legal question here is..."

The point of the article, "What's So Funny About Death and Inheritance" was to give "estate planners" some idea of the confusion in the minds of the common citizen arising through the complications of normal life and the fact no one ever taught Baby Boomers about inheritance, death, or planning anything about it.

It is appropriate to present these questions at the beginning of this book so you can start thinking about them so the answers become clear during your reading. Therefore:

"It was on the January 2, 2006 *Good Morning America* show I first heard that over 7,000 Americans would turn 60 years old every day of the year in 2006. They claimed there were over 80 million Baby Boomers in this country, and consequently, from that morning on, not a single show would go by without some mention of the "Baby Boomer" phenomena for quite some time. The interest seems to have waned, or people have simply gotten used-to the aging problems in 2008 now that 7,000 Americans are going to be turning 65 years old every day and going on Medicaid. Today's bad news is there are not sufficient resources to handle it.

What came to my mind was: How many of these Baby Boomers know what a Bypass Trust is, or a QTIP Trust? Thinking of all this amassed wealth held by these Baby Boomers, I wondered how many knew what would happen to their children's inheritance if the surviving spouse remarried and there was no "Credit Shelter Trust" to protect the children's interest. And what about their adult children from a previous marriage? Do they have their inheritance protected?

Do these Baby Boomers know not all their amassed wealth is community property? Do they know who has the right to give what property to whom? Have they ever thought about a transmutation agreement? Have they talked? Are they aware that under California Family Code § 721 they must communicate truthfully with each other? Do they know the tax benefit of transmuting joint tenancy property into community property? Do they know the repercussions?

What makes this funny to me is that I was a personal injury attorney in Santa Barbara for over 20 years and I couldn't answer those questions either, not without studying the subject. So what chance does the common Baby Boomer have to benefit from the tools of estate planning if someone doesn't explain it to them in plain language? It would cost them dearly for a lawyer's time to tell them what they probably can't understand without flow charts anyway. It is a difficult subject.

Since we don't live in the ideal attorney's world, where a couple starts planning for divorce immediately upon getting married, a typical couple works hard and commingles assets with little regard toward the characterization of their property and how the title is held, such as separate, community, or quasi-community.

But if, after careful consideration, a couple had decided to convert their separate property into community property, then a transmutation agreement acknowledging that new ownership can be of great benefit. A transmutation agreement is where both couples agree in writing to change the characterization of their property from one characterization to another, e.g., private property to community property.

But *Beware!* As shown below, an agreement converting separate property into community property is the first thing they will want to revoke when considering divorce. Otherwise, and that is a big otherwise, it is a good tool for a well planned estate and greatly enhances the property rights of the surviving spouse.

Assume an attorney encourages a couple married for twenty-five years to transmute the ownership of their residence from "joint tenancy with right of survivorship" into community property so they can gain a tax advantage at the death of the first spouse for the surviving spouse.

For example, if the couple purchased a home in 1986 for $600,000 and in 2006 the home was worth $2 million (not uncommon in California), each of the couple's half (50%) of the cost basis would be $300,000 (1/2 of $600,000 is $300,000).

If the husband died, and the property was still held in joint tenancy, his 50% of the cost basis ($300,000) would "step up" to $1 million (50% fair market value at the time of death which is now $2 million total) but the wife's cost basis would remain at $300,000 (her 50% share would not "step up" to the current fair market value of $2 million.)

Consequently, if the wife sold the property immediately after her husband's death she would pay capital gains taxes on $700,000, (that is the capital gains on her 50% share of the fair market value of $2 million). Since her cost basis is $300,000, that leaves $700,000 to be taxed federally at 15% for capital gain, and 9% for California State capital gain tax. Her total tax at 24% equals $168,000 to the government.

Because the couple left their property in *joint tenancy,* the survivor received only a 50% step-up when the first spouse died and paid taxes on $700,000, equaling $168,000, when she sold the home for $2 million.

But if the couple had entered into a transmutation agreement converting ownership of the residence to community property, then upon her husband's death, her 50% cost basis would "step up" to $1 million, the same as her husband's "stepped up" to $1 million. With a combined cost basis of $2 million, there would be no recognized capital gains and she would pay no taxes if she decided to sell!

This would be wise estate planning in the event of death, but what if the couple was getting divorced the next year and the husband died before the divorce and before he could revoke the transmutation? Would his attorney get sued for malpractice by the husband's heirs for persuading the couple to form a transmutation agreement in the first place?"

The article goes on, but that is enough questions for now and we would be getting ahead of ourselves. Let's start planning your estate distribution NOW.

CHAPTER FIVE

First, Create a Vision

Needless to say, you cannot create a vision without first knowing what you are creating a vision about. In this case, the vision is about everything you own and how you want to give it away after you die. This could be an easy job for the married couple who had nothing of value before they got married, and the first spouse to die plans on leaving everything to the surviving spouse and their children, if they have any.

But we are talking about doing this the right way, the way George Washington would have done it, so each item would need to be commemorated and specified who it would go to. This is not how it is most commonly done in Revocable Trust or Wills today. All material goods are normally lumped under one heading such as "Tangible Personal Property," which refers to furniture and furnishings, silverware, objects of art, china, clothing, jewelry, sporting equipment, automobiles, books, collections of tangible goods, and any other tangible goods that are "to be shared equally, share and share alike" by the children, or some such phraseology.

Now think for two seconds how helpful that is to the three children drooling over the audio-visual equipment, restored Mustang, or ski boat.

If it is difficult for you to decide, and come up with a reason why, think how difficult it will be for them to decide amongst themselves. You are supposed to be much older and wiser. It is also these types of sibling disputes which end up back in probate court for a judge's decision.

George and Martha Washington, by the way, had no children, so he was forced to think long and hard about what family members and charities he wished to benefit. He had only two step-children from Martha's previous marriage. The daughter, Patsy, died as a teenager at Mt Vernon, and the son, John, died in 1781 in an army hospital, leaving five children. That makes his situation very similar to today's concept of the "blended family." Nevertheless, Mr. Washington took stock in everything he owned and recorded it in his "schedule of property," along with its appraised value.

However, that is one of the problems with Wills. You would not want your version of the appraised value to fall into the hands of the court. If you chose the path of the Last Will and Testament, the probate fee will be determined by a probate referee, based on the appraised value of the estate. The appraised value of any item includes the amount of money still owing on it. It is not appraised at the estate's net value, but at its gross value. This is an issue we will review when discussing the advantages and disadvantages of a Revocable Trust.

But in regard to specifying to whom your tangible goods will go, George Washington's dilemma involved, for one example, the numerous swords he had been given or had used in famous battles, the honor bestowed upon it, a comment as to how the sword should be used by the new owner, as well as the name of the person to whom it shall be given. Another of his problems was dividing up the numerous parcels of land he was paid as a surveyor during his youth in the western territories, along with the land grants that traditionally came to an officer for military service.

In our time, for the average person to divvy up his, or her, tangible goods around the house, or other properties he may own, there is no reason to believe the gifts are any less genuine and loving as those in Washington's family. It may be the electrical tools, or Eagle Scout badge, or restored muscle cars, varsity jackets, suits, shoes, old science projects, lucky stones, a certain writing desk, or any other utensil. The list is endless, and the same goes for Mrs. Smith and her dolls, dresses, salt and pepper shaker collection, sewing machines, or sub-machine gun collection for all I know.

The point is, before a wife and husband can seriously take on the task of giving away their estate they each need to know what they have. This is not a project that needs to be done together. In fact, in privacy with time to think would most likely be the best choice.

But, of course these are all the small personal items of minimum value that neither spouse probably really cares what the other one does with it. In most cases, these items have already been cleared as the domain of the other spouse. But you can be certain that every person who receives a special token is going to treasure the item forever. A grandfather giving a painting of a ship to his grandson could lead to a life of high seas adventure. You just never know the impact of the statement. It is worth thinking about and easy to do, in fact, even fun to do.

What seems to bog the vision down is when it comes to items of substantial value, such as real estate, and prior holdings that are dubious as to whether they are separate or community property. Many people who know that certain property is their separate property are reluctant to say so, for fear of sounding greedy.

What seems like a million dollars to one person may be only ten thousand dollars to another. But when it really does involve a million dollars, there are competing interests that make the job of distribution very difficult because of the various personalities.

In the Appendix of this book, you will find a general questionnaire to learn about who you and your spouse are, and exactly who believes they own how big a portion of the property you both share. It is recommended this form be used as an outline to start a conversation you should have at the dinner table when no one else is around. It may turn out you do not agree on some of the items, but it will give you the range and character of the property that must be analyzed.

Just because you do not agree on one or two subjects does not mean there is no room for compromise. Once again, remind yourself if it is difficult for the two of you to agree, how will your children do if they are left to split the property? Regardless of ownership, you may be able to agree on when it will be a gift. It is a job that has to be done, and most likely you will not disagree because ultimately you want to be fair with each other. But as I have said, this seems to be a stumbling block that can bog down the vision for many couples.

Remember, what you are doing is a good, generous and responsible act that is going to create much happiness. All those heirs receiving gifts are getting something for just being born. How could they possibly complain about your decision on how to split up your own property? To a certain extent it exhibits how you want to be remembered. Just do your best to be fair by placing yourself in the other person's shoes.

Or, you could simply be pragmatic. Write what properties are under your control and split them down the middle. But you cannot begrudge your husband or wife because they got an inheritance, making it their separate property and maintained their sole right to dispose of it. Nor can you begrudge your spouse if they came into the marriage with more than you. Remember George Washington married one of the richest widows in the Colonies, and wrote his Will in his own hand the same as you could. (Make sure you sign and date each page to fulfill the requirements of a Holographic Will.)

The first item on Washington's list of priorities was that his debts be paid "punctually and speedily." His second priority was that his "beloved wife Martha" be given his whole estate "for the term of her natural life." Third was the emancipation of his slaves upon her death, only waiting because his slaves were interbred with her slaves and that would result in chaos for Martha in the last years of her life. As stated, he was an exact man of deliberate thought.

A Problem We Should All Have, or Not

For example, take a 65 year-old man who just inherited $3 million from his mother. Her husband purchased ranch land for $2.00 an acre 75 years ago. Now each acre is worth $25,000, with subdivisions and shopping centers rising from the oasis surrounding the property. The fact that the son inherited it from his mother makes it his separate property to bequeath or give away to whomever he wants. The wife has no legal say in the matter, but she has plenty to say as a wife.

The problem is the 65 year-old man and his wife have no children, and the man has no blood lineage left to whom he wants to give his fortune, nor any charity. But the wife has a niece with whom she is very close. The niece is her twin sister's daughter, but this daughter dropped out of high school and has been in and out of rehab and jail for a hard narcotic habit. She has been like this for several years, but the wife believes the young lady will soon grow up and accept responsibility and made something of her life. The husband is extremely doubtful she will grow up to do anything.

Added to this twisted situation, the wife fully expects the money to go to her niece because the husband has failed to tell her there is not a chance in hell of that happening. He does not tell her because he knows his wife will freak out when she hears this and his life will become miserable.

What are they to do? They cannot continuously not talk about it, because if the husband does not put it in some kind of trust (which we will talk about later), or give it to someone else, which would end their marriage (the happy one anyway), then the money will all go to his wife anyway, assuming he dies first. Consequently, she will leave it to the niece when she dies, despite her husband's sentiments.

Perhaps we should all have the problem of worrying how to give away three million dollars. But do not forget this was his family's money. Who ends up with the money means a lot to him, and if it ends up in a drug dealer's hands, it would make the husband roll over in his grave. In fact, it may make him come out of his grave.

Had they read this book, it would open their vision to at least ten good ways to split up that money into a trust or trusts, so everyone would feel good and justified about the outcome. He could put any number of limitations on a trust outlining the niece's behavior before she would ever get a dime.

This is an introduction into what are called "trusts." There are many kinds that are tax saving, easily controlled, and only limited by your imagination, and the rules of the IRS.

Your own conversational problems with your spouse in creating a vision for distribution may be far different from the example given above, but it still comes down to having a honest conversation on how to split up the estate. You are in this together, one way or the other. As stated over and over, the more you know about trusts, trustees, the meaning of the non-marital tax deduction and so much more, the more it will help you realize you are not trapped in a one solution problem, even with a small estate. Plus, there is always the option of spending all the money and leaving nothing behind. The idea is to enjoy life.

Keep Your Family Business Honest

In California there is a law codified in California Family Code §721 which actually creates a fiduciary duty between a man and wife obligating them to communicate truthfully.

What a concept! This is something the law has developed to help balance any business acumen or financial advantage one spouse may have over the other. It helps regulate their confidential relationship regarding community property transactions between themselves. For example, suppose Husband wants to leave the family residence to a daughter from a previous marriage, including Wife's community share without discussing with her the right he knows she has to give away her share of the house to anyone she wants?

The Husband's fiduciary duty to his Wife, and vice versa, is the same as that fiduciary relationship between general business partners in their business activities. The husband must explain to his wife what he wants to do, and do so by putting the plan in order without putting Wife's estate at an unfair disadvantage. In this instance he could give her another piece of his separate property to even out the deal. If Wife is okay with giving up her share of the residence, then she must put it in writing. Otherwise the gift would be voidable, meaning the wife could go to court to have the gift to the daughter voided so the wife could stay in the home.

This duty, codified in California in § 721, is the same principle recognized in any contract where one party has the duty to be truthful about the facts and failed to do so. That person is guilty of fraud if he knew of the truth and intended to benefit by not sharing it with his partner. The duty of honesty between husband and wife to give true and accurate information regarding anything that affects their community property transaction is imposed in every state, but it can really be ugly for the whole family in probate court as well as expensive. It imposes a duty of the "highest good faith," and few judges don't hold it in the highest regard. That is another good reason for avoiding probate court.

However, under this law, it means if there is any "Agreement" between spouses that the court deems unfair to one, the Agreement is presumed to be a breach of their spousal duty and can be undone through legal action. So unless you hate your spouse, in which case you should get a divorce, follow Ben Franklin's advice that "honesty is the best policy."

As discussed above, a couple's priorities and property "characterization" must be discussed before anything else can be planned, and it must be discussed openly and honestly so there are no problems that raise their ugly head later in the properly distributed process amongst the heirs.

These issues of "priorities" must first be discussed with your spouse, and then the spouses must somehow communicate their wishes precisely to an attorney to put in legal order. Because this communication process is sometimes flawed for lack of understanding or misuse of terms, there are estate planning advisors who work with a team of tax, insurance, investment and charity experts who will review your Revocable Trust to make certain the trust will indeed work the way you want it to.

These are not always easy subjects to discuss because it may sound selfish identifying your separate property as your own. But it is absolutely necessary to characterize your property as separate in order to determine who can give what to whom, as an individual gift. If not, it could be successfully contested by an heir in court which is exactly what you wanted to avoid.

Not everything is community property, as you should now be well aware! The inheritance you received years back, or the house you bought before marriage, or the painting from your brother, is your separate property. Your attorney or advisor can be very helpful in bringing these issues out for discussion by offering a dispassionate analysis of the title to these goods along with the pros and cons if you find yourself in a stalemate with your partner.

Some of the other questions couples need to discuss are:

1. Will you need separate representation?
2. Is there a prenuptial agreement to consider?
3. What are your tax objectives?
4. How will, or can, life insurance affect your estate?
5. Who will be trustee - spouse, friend, professional?
6. Should a surviving spouse be sole trustee for the Credit Shelter Trust?
7. Who will be guardian of your children? And, who will handle their funds?
8. Who gets the "family heirlooms?"
9. Are there clear lines of communication between your current spouse and your children from your previous marriages?
10. Are you speaking truthfully about exactly what you expect, or are you presuming what to expect?

Once this type of dialogue is underway, you can begin connecting the dots between your priorities with legal tools which are designed to do the job that meets your priorities.

Have a Strong Work Ethic for Your Vision

Early to bed and early to rise, makes a man healthy, wealthy... and finishes his estate plan?

We are not talking "work ethic" in the Puritanical sense here. But in all honesty, it does take a sense of "hard nose to grindstone," (as my father use to say) to get the job done, otherwise it stays where it is today, in perpetual procrastination.

As far as getting up at sunrise is concerned, it personally puts me in a nasty mood. But it was often said of George Washington that he rose with the sun and expected everyone who worked for him to do the same. If you think you are busy, *forget about it,* when it comes to George Washington.

Even at age 65, he was riding his horse in the wee hours of the morning across hill and dale of his vast 8,000 acres that made up the five different farms known as Mt. Vernon. His intent was to make certain everyone was working, rather than face the alternative of being fired for not laboring when and where they were supposed to be (or what he called their "indisposition"). He would be back at the mansion for breakfast with the inevitable guest by seven o'clock.

Washington had always been the man who led by example. It is safe to say he was a workaholic. In the eight years of the Revolutionary war he never took a vacation, and only visited Mt. Vernon ten days out of the entire eight years of war. Mt. Vernon suffered from his absence, but at least the land upon which the estate rested was purchased by young George Washington with "futures" on his tobacco crops that were lent to him by the English banks he defeated in the Revolutionary War. That is one way to settle a debt.

But Washington's absence left plenty of work to be done on the farms both in management and back breaking labor, even after his two terms of presidency were over. He undertook all the management himself. And yet, it is estimated he wrote 20,000 letters over his life. That is enough to fill the 90 volumes which were collected by the University of Virginia. Where did he find the time? It certainly puts Ronald Reagan's book, *The Reagan Diaries,* in perspective.

In regards to Washington's own management of Mt. Vernon, it applies to you in a different way. It is only you who can go about managing the creation of a proper estate plan for your family. Washington could have left all management of the farm to a foreman or two, the same way so many people want to leave their estate plan to be done by an attorney who does not know them, then accepts his judgment on blind faith, not even understanding what the attorney is talking about.

This blind delegation of duty by property owners is wrong. Yet it is often done, even though they do not understand what a Revocable Trust really is or how it works, and with no skepticism that the attorney creating the plan could make a mistake, or actually use a one-size-fits-all boilerplate form, but they do it anyway. They just feel good it is done, as long as they did not have to pay too much for it. I am sorry to have to say that, but it has always amazed me how a person who works 45 years to reach his or her retirement and to build their estate, only wants to spend a couple of hours preparing the plan on who to leave the estate, and then puts the responsibility onto a complete stranger.

Practically speaking, an estate plan is not a difficult task to perform. It could actually be thought of as fun and creative if you put it in the proper perspective. After all, it actually is your work, and not the work of the person you are doing it for. In the words of Mark Twain, "The work that is really a man's own work is play and not work at all."

Once you have listed all of the tangible goods you own, along with your real estate, and decided which of those persons or charities you wish to give these gifts to, then it only takes creating they way you are going to give it to your heirs. You do not want them to pay the 45% tax if your estate is presently over $2 million, and in 2009 it will be 45% over $3.5 million.

I am sure the general public might think this estate tax has no application to them because their estate is presently only worth $500,000, and the economy is on the *kaput.* But ask yourself if you think you are going to die in the next two years, and if not, remember the estate tax law will drastically change in 2010. At the very least, and absent any intervening tax legislation the estate tax will revert back to 50% over $1 million in 2011. Then ask yourself what will happen if you accidentally live 20 or 30 years longer and your estate continues to grow?

Let's face it. Probably 100% of you reading this book are going to live longer than the next two years unless a tragic accident occurs, in which case you damn well better have an estate plan in place. (Those left behind will be sorrowful enough.) The only thing you are missing to formulate the vision, after the list of gifts and the recipients, is the glue that holds the whole thing together. This is what the estate planning business calls, "Credit Shelter Trusts."

However, you cannot learn about Credit Shelter Trusts without first understanding the system they operate within. I call that the "Death and Inheritance System," but it is normally referred to as "probate." To understand it we must start at the beginning.

CHAPTER SIX

What Is Probate?

From an attorney's point of view, there are two kinds of potential clients who have preconceived notions about probate and the role of estate planning. Some people believe everything they have heard or perhaps read about a Living Trust, otherwise known as a Revocable Trust, and how it avoids probate. Therefore, it must be good because you don't have to pay all those fees, particularly to the attorney.

It is these people who think this type of trust is so simple they can do it themselves, or expect it to be so commonplace that they can buy a one-size-fits-all boilerplate form at wholesale prices from a trust mill, and get their money's worth...and they do. They believe whatever they are told about holding these unknown probate fees to the minimum, including the salesman's assurance the Living Trust is right for them and for everybody else too, because it avoids probate.

This is not true, so dispel that thought from your mind. The ironic truth is that these like-thinkers will be the first ones back in probate court because the job was not done right. Their heirs do not know what to do, so they will seek an attorney who must now take it into probate court in order to iron out the problems with the judge.

So the last thing these victims of Living Trust mills wanted ends up being the first thing they get, or more appropriately, the first things their heirs get.

The second kinds of people are the kind who read this book in order to understand the parts of the system and how it works. They can then use professional help, after which they are prepared to speak intelligently on the subject, and know what they want.

Many people do not really understand what "probate" is. When we speak of "probate" we are talking about a specialized legal procedure that takes place at the courthouse, and is governed by the laws in the "Probate Code." As stated earlier, California is one of thirty-two states who have not adopted even a modified version of the "Uniform Probate Code," so you can be certain the laws are quite different in those thirty-two states. Probate court is where all Last Will and Testaments are petitioned for and administrated under the jurisdiction of the court.

Probate court does not mean it is a court found in a different location than your local superior court, or whatever the highest court in your county is called. It can be located in the same courtroom where the same judge may also preside over a civil case involving a car accident, or a criminal case involving a murder. Probate court can be in the same place you go to dispute a contract over the lower court's jurisdictional limit.

Probate begins when a "petition" is filed with the court asking the judge's permission to do certain things such as obtain "Letters Testamentary." These Letters allow the executor to gain access to banks and other financial institutions, file tax returns, collect personal property and manage the estate assets, to name just a few.

A "probate referee" who works for the state government will be assigned to appraise the value of the estate. In California the referee is paid 1% of the gross appraised value for their services. Remember that the "gross" value pays no attention to the amount of money owed on it. That value is what determines the probate fee for administration of your Will as shown in the chart below.

After an inventory and accounting of the estate is approved by the court, and approximately 15 to 24 months later, the executor can make the final distribution of the estate assets to the heirs, in accordance with the Will. Of course, any number of legal conflicts can occur between when the Letters Testamentary are issued and final distribution of the assets to the heirs. These conflicts can cause "extraordinary fees" to be paid to the attorney and/or executor out of the estate.

Below is a table depicting the superior court's filing fees in the State of California. Again, the estate value is determined by the "gross" size of your estate, not the "net." Therefore, it does not include the debt which is owed on any tangible or real property.

Size of Estate	Court Filing Fee
Under $250,000	**$233.50**
$250,000	**$305.00**
$500,000	**$415.00**
$750,000	**$580.00**
$1,000,000	**$1,130.00**
$1,500,000	**$2,230.00**
$2,000,000	**$2,780.00**
$2,500,000	**$3,880.00**

According to this table, if an estate is valued at $1.5 million, the court filing fee will be $2,230. If it is under $250,000 the fee will be $233.50.

Probate court is not just for administrating Wills. It has jurisdiction over guardians and conservatorships, trust administration, powers of attorney, health care decisions, and many other issues.

Avoiding Probate

One of the reasons for first creating a vision of what you want is to help you determine whether you actually need a Revocable Trust, or only want one to avoid your preconceived nightmare about probate.

The Revocable Trust will help you to avoid probate, but there is a secondary benefit that may be considered more important than the cost savings. Avoiding probate means you are ensuring your right to privacy. Avoiding probate is like avoiding a long line at the Department of Motor Vehicles, or at the post office, but in probate court everyone can look inside your package.

When your estate is in probate, it can be examined through the court records by any member of public who may have an interest in your affairs. There is no right to privacy. Your estate, its value and your plan will be scrutinized by members of the court staff, including the probate referee, the judge, any attorney, or perhaps an ombudsman from a governmental agency who feels it their duty to interfere with your family affairs.

There are many probate cases where the court's investigative eyes might be essential to the fair administration of a Last Will and Testament. This is particularly true when there is no executor you can trust to handle the administration of the Will correctly. In the case of a Revocable Trust, it is the Trustee who has the duty to administer the Trust outside the eyes of probate. But it is the executor of a Will who has the duty of hiring an attorney and attending to several other duties which will be discussed later.

But if you do not want your affairs open to neighbors, creditors, business associates, long lost relatives, or simply the curious, then avoiding probate has a value beyond that of saving money. Better yet is the fact a Revocable Trust can help you avoid the indignity of having a conservator appointed to take care of you if you become disabled or incompetent. If you already have someone, or two, who you would prefer to take over the management of your life, a Revocable Trust is the best way to go.

Show Me the Money

It is going to cost you about the same, or perhaps more money up front, to have a Revocable Trust tailored to your vision than a Will. That is because the attorney makes his money on the back end after a Will has been administrated. But it takes the same skills to write a tailor made Trust as it does a Will.

Whether the decedent (the person who died) has a Will or not, if the entire value of the estate, including real and personal property, does not exceed $100,000, (in California) and the heir to the estate is readily identifiable, then the property can be collected and distributed without the need for probate administration (The value of the estate excludes joint tenancies, IRAs, insurance policies, 401(k)...).

The heir or beneficiary can obtain their interest in personal property by using an affidavit or declaration alone. In order to accomplish the transfer of real property, the heir or beneficiary must file a declaration and petition to the court requesting the estate's real property be conveyed to them. Does that sound easy? If so, just follow the instructions beginning at Division 8 of the California Probate Code. I am sure there are like provisions in every other state.

The Probate Code also offers a family protection plan for the small estate whereby the surviving spouse and minor children can petition the court to have the family homestead "set aside" in order to protect it from creditors.

If the net value of the decedent's entire estate does not exceed $20,000 (over and above all liens and encumbrances including the probate homestead) then a petition may be filed to have the estate "set aside." This, in effect, is permission from a judge to be excused from probate (California Probate Code § 6600).

Therefore, if your estate, or that which you are entitled to by right of succession, is less than $100,000, for a nominal fee you can give your paperwork to an attorney and have him/her draw up the papers "setting aside" the estate.

For all those Wills which are not excused from probate, much ado is made about the cost of paying attorney fees. These fees are regulated by statute and there is little argument that a huge estate valued at millions of dollars will carry a huge attorney fee, because it is based on a percentage of the estate's value.

But little is ever said about the personal representative, called the "executor," who receives exactly the same compensation for his services as the attorney. Any executor has a right to waive this fee for the benefit of the other heirs to the estate, but this author has never met one, but that does not mean they do not exist. It would make them a hero, or maybe just a person who does not need the money.

In fact, the personal representative's duty normally begins by hiring an attorney, and then essentially becomes the attorney's helper. It is anticipated the executor is familiar with the estate and will act as liaison between family business and legal business.

In order for you to determine if these attorney and executor fees are reasonable, the scale for compensation in California, based on the appraised value of the estate, is as follows:

1. 4% on the first $100,000;
2. 3% on the next $100,000;
3. 2% on the next $800,000;
4. 1% on the next $9,000,000;
5. ½% on the next $15,000,000;
6. For estates above $25,000,000 a reasonable fee will be determined by the court.

Estate Value	Statutory Fee
$100,000	$4,000
$200,000	$7,000
$300,000	$9,000
$400,000	$11,000
$500,000	$13,000
$600,000	$15,000
$700,000	$17,000
$800,000	$19,000
$900,000	$21,000
$1,000,000	$23,000
$2,000,000	$33,000

Based on this scale, the compensation paid to the attorney and the executor on a $1.5 million dollar estate is $28,000 each, for a total of $56,000. On an estate of $500,000, the attorney and the executor would each receive $13,000. Is it worth it?

When we take up the subject of trustees in Chapter Eight, it may be the deciding factor whether you believe you need the court to oversee the administration of your estate. If you have a responsible person to act as trustee who will accept whatever the demands of your particular estate may be, then you are in good shape.

The Best Reason to Avoid Probate

Now that you know what Probate is, along with its function and the associated fees, you have a reality check on if it is right for you. You have also been warned about a "Conservatorship" without any details behind the warning.

Not enough emphasis can be put on this subject, especially if you are unaware of the prospects and the resulting rules of management over the person who becomes the Conservatee. You also need to know that even though the original intentions behind initiating a "Petition for Conservatorship" over someone you love may appear obviously "just" to you, they can turn out horribly unfair. An examination of the process may be a very practical way to convince you to stay out of probate court and use a Revocable Trust as a substitute for a "conservatorship." It may be your only reason for having a Revocable Trust in many cases.

Not only is a conservatorship proceeding expensive for your estate, but it pits many competing family members, government agencies and financial entities against each other in order to gain control over your assets through the court system. These competing interests range from errant relatives to court appointed "professional" conservators. These professional conservators, and their entourage of health care providers and financial assistants, can be a disease on your estate. These are situations you want to avoid like the plague.

For a startling review of the subject, look up the excellent journalistic exposé of the private world of conservators and guardians that ran in the *Los Angeles Times* beginning November 13, 2005. These four articles, written on consecutive Sundays, investigate the unsupervised world of court-ordered professional caregivers, and reveal the rampant abuse of the elderly who these "professionals" are ordered to protect. The series is available for free on-line at your local library. The articles were the impetus behind Governor Schwarzenegger's signing, on September 27, 2007, The Omnibus Conservatorship and Guardian Reform Act of 2006, that took effect on July 1, 2007.

The *Los Angeles Times'* articles about professional conservators exposed facts which brought such heart wrenching descriptions of neglect, incompetence, abuse, and lack of oversight by the judicial system, it actually moved the state assembly into doing something about it.

As of July 1, 2008, the definition of professional fiduciary will be expanded beyond conservators and guardians to include trustees, agents under a durable power of attorney for health care and agents under power of attorney for finance. This means hundreds of individuals, who never intended to be professionals, will now be "professional fiduciaries" and therefore liable under a much higher standard of duty to their client.

Therefore, the one thing you definitely want to avoid is subjecting yourself and your family to the humiliation of having a conservator assigned to manage your person and your property. First, understand a conservator means a stranger who manages every minute of your day, and every penny of your money.

If you become incapacitated and have not directly addressed the issue of who will govern your estate, it will be a starting gun for the named competitive interests to gain control over the estate, particularly where a blended family is involved. This is something to be concerned about because not only can a wayward daughter or stepchild initiate court proceedings against your wife or husband for a conservatorship, but outside interests, such as banks, security companies, and money management firms may also get involved. In fact, they may believe it is their duty to get involved, and in all fairness, in some cases that may be true.

But in other cases, these so-called fiduciaries will contact elder law personnel who can then pounce on your estate with a flurry of accusations of abuse, and they can do so regardless of the truth. The next thing you know, after ~~a~~ huge expenses defending these false claims against the caregiver, a judge will appoint an unknown professional conservator, at an incredulously high price to your estate, to manage your family's every move.

Here is an anecdotal story where all the names have been changed to protect the innocent. This is what happened to Dr. X and his wife Wilma:

Dr. X was an emergency room physician who had been married to Wilma for 26 years. They both had daughters from previous marriages, Anna and Beatrice, who had gotten along well during their teenage years, before moving out and going their separate ways. Wilma continued to take care of her husband as best as any wife can do.

In his late seventies the doctor began to exhibit signs of Alzheimer's and deteriorated quickly. He could no longer manage his estate and Wilma did the best she could with what little knowledge she had about his financial holdings. She could certainly balance a check book and knew the needs of running the house she had lived in and managed for 26 years.

Before long the doctor's daughter, Anna, who recently had very little presence in the home, began coming by more often and taking items of value from the home. Because she believed, or so she represented, that she was to inherit the house when her father died, Anna somehow finagled personal contacts at the bank to release large sums of estate money for her to use to remodel the family home.

About this time Wilma was diagnosed with an early stage of breast cancer and began undergoing treatment, from which she fully recovered. Her daughter from her former marriage, Beatrice, a doctor herself, came home from Arizona to help take care of her mother and Dr. X, her step-father. This is when all hell broke loose.

Anna began a verbal attack on Wilma for not being able to properly care for her father, and accused her step-sister Beatrice of imposing on the family home and being a leech on her mother, which meant to Anna a leech on her potential inheritance. Even though Anna, as Dr. X's daughter, is not by law the favored relative to be appointed as her father's conservator, she nevertheless petitioned the court for the appointment so she could gain control over his estate.

Ironically, by law the first person to be considered the best conservator for Dr. X, or any other incapacitated husband, is his wife, which in this case was Wilma.

Unfortunately for Wilma, Anna's vicious personal attacks and unfounded lies about Wilma's incompetence, and Beatrice's hidden agenda to leech off the estate, were heard by the court. Anna sought alliance from her friends at the bank, and got it in the form of adjoining legal counsel, if only to protect the bank's interest because they were holding the doctor's money in trust.

Based on the above information the judge decided to:

- Assign a court appointed attorney to represent the incompetent Dr. X;
- Order a professional conservator to be appointed by the court attorney;
- Order health care providers to live in the family home 24 hours a day;
- Order every penny that Wilma spent to be authorized by a bank trustee;
- Order Beatrice and Anna restrained from the family home; and

- Order strict visiting hours for Beatrice and Anna to visit their mother and father at their family home.

In this example it should come as no surprise that the court appointed attorney, the conservator, the health care provider service and the bank trustee were all friends, and each extracted large fees from Dr. X's estate.

Take this into consideration if deciding whether a Revocable Trust is not worth it. In some cases, avoiding conservatorship is the only reason that makes it worth it.

CHAPTER SEVEN

The Smaller Estate

A friendly line of questioning for any husband about estate planning is: "You love your wife, right? And if you died tomorrow, you would want her to move on in life, right? But would you want her new husband to have access to your half of the community property you worked for your entire life, or would you rather it be preserved for your minor (adult) children?"

The most prevalent answer has been that the man would rather preserve his half of community property for his children. Their half of community property is the same as separate property. What they don't understand is that preserving their half of the estate for their children from a previous marriage does not happen without them doing something about it.

Most Baby Boomers do not even know they can give away their half of community property. To do so they must craft a Revocable Trust (also known as a Living Trust) or Will that funds an irrevocable trust upon their death. This trust provides benefits to the surviving spouse during his or her lifetime, but the remainder goes to the children at a certain age. What age and how much is the subject of discussion.

The point is the value of your estate cannot be measured in dollars alone. It is easy to preserve what you want for your children when you are gone, as long as you do it before you leave. It is not hard to learn the basics of the system, and all the estate planning tools available to the very rich are just as available to the smaller estates. It just involves smaller amounts of assets.

The first question in any estate planning is whether or not your estate will be subject to federal estate taxes upon your death. This is determined by the gross value (not the net) of your estate at the time you die. This estate value at the time of death is speculated in advance by examining your age and annual income, your present assets with growth potential, your expectation of inheritance, your health care needs, your business acumen, etc. How this information applies to the estate tax after 2010 will depend on what the new administration does.

In the year of 2008, the federal estate tax begins at $2 million. This means if your (or your parents') estate is valued at $2 million or less, and you or they die in '08, the estate will pay no federal estate taxes. But if your estate is worth $2.5 million and you die in 2008, it will be taxed on the overage of $500,000 at 45% tax. If you die a year later in 2009, this exemption amount changes to $3.5 million, and your estate will be taxed on any amount over $3.5 million, at 45%. Please see the table below.

YEAR	AMOUNT EXEMPT FROM ESTATE TAX	HIGHEST TAX BRACKET
2001	$675,000	55%
2002	$1,000,000	50%
2003	$1,000,000	49%
2004	$1,500,000	48%
2005	$1,500,000	47%
2006	$2,000,000	46%
2007	$2,000,000	45%
2008	$2,000,000	45%
2009	$3,500,000	45%
2010	Unlimited	N/A
2011	Reverts to $1,000,000 unless there is intervening legislation.	

(This table will be examined and discussed in detail in Chapter Ten.)

Once you have determined to whom you want to give your money, the second thing estate planning is all about is not giving your money to the government. After all, you already paid taxes on most of that earned income. You do not want your heirs to pay taxes again at a rate of 45% when you die.

Assuming your estate is under $2 million in 2008 and thus exempt from taxes, it may be possible to plan its administration using either a Will or a Revocable Trust. (A Revocable Trust always comes with a Pourover Will, but that's another story). Planning for this smaller estate is relatively simple, and probate cost and attorney fees can be avoided or be minimal when a client's desires are "traditional."

The tools for estate planning become more complicated when the scenario changes to blended families with children young and old, shared or visiting, with ex-spouses and/or premature deaths, contested community property, business partnerships, hazy ownerships and other individual considerations. This makes it more difficult to sort out what plan would be best.

Once each spouse's assets are identified, it must be determined how to distribute them. For example, is it better to hold ownership of your real property with your wife in joint tenancy with right of survivorship, or should you have a transmutation agreement converting the property to community property? Transmutation is a great idea if you remain married because it will "step-up" the value of the entire property to the fair market value if the surviving spouse decides to sell. He or she would pay no capital gains. But a transmutation agreement is the first thing you want to revoke if you even begin thinking of divorce.

Instead of leaving money to the children upon your death, should a "Family Pot Trust" be created so as not to distribute the entire sum of money until the youngest child reaches a certain age? And if you have a disabled child, perhaps a

Special Needs Trust is appropriate. As shown above, you want to avoid a court appointed conservatorship if it is possible, and a Revocable Trust is good for that if nothing else.

There are many important decisions a husband and wife must make for estate planning which requires them to talk openly and truthfully about their feelings. What happens when the first spouse dies? Where will his or her separate property go? How will the step-up in estate value affect the surviving spouse? Will a Bypass Trust (also known by many other names) be necessary? What happens if a spouse remarries? What about a guardian? Who will be trustee?

One of the shortcomings of a Will is that when both parents are gone the assets of the estate are generally given outright to the children if they are eighteen or older. Some of them may not be ready to manage this windfall profit and would greatly benefit from a trust that controls the timing of the distributions.

There are many trusts and trustees to choose from to help guide children until they reach a certain age. A trust for the children's benefit can be very flexible, or not, depending on the desired goal. Would it be only for their education? Would it be distributed at ages twenty, twenty-six and thirty? Could they buy a car at age eighteen? What exactly would it mean to provide funds for their needs? Which needs?

If the trustee is your wife, or favorite son or daughter, which may be fine, but are they equipped to follow the legal discipline governing a trustee's "fiduciary duty?" Your daughter may be great at making money, but that doesn't prepare her for preserving capital or distributing your funds according to other sibling's needs, particularly if those brothers and sisters are from a "blended family."

The value of a good trustee cannot be overstated. A trustee has the highest fiduciary duty prescribed by law, meaning he or she must act with well intentioned reason and sound judgment regarding your affairs at all times. The trustee is given serious responsibility to look after the best interest of people ranging from minor children to disabled grandparents. This is often in exchange for very little payment, even though potentially they could be managing hundreds of thousands of dollars in the trust.

Therefore, you must decide who the right person is for the job. It is not the same as choosing a guardian for your children. Guardians are chosen because of their loving nature, their shared moral integrity, their ability and willingness to accept your child or children into their house, financial wherewithal to provide for additional children, the size of their house, the town, the school, and their ambient family nature.

Would you allow a stranger to choose a babysitter for your kids? You may name a guardian in your Will or Trust which the judge should consider seriously when he appoints a guardian. If there are competing parties, the judge will decide who will be guardian according to what he perceives as the best interest of the child.

Although these options can be overwhelming at first, particularly in light of impending mortality, you can rest assured a well planned estate is the best gift you can leave your heirs. Estate planning is not an unnecessary expense; it is a positive and virtuous legacy used to avoid chaos after a lifetime of work. With sound legal advice and knowledgeable tactics you can provide yourself and loved ones a great feeling of security.

There is no cookie cutter, one-size-fits-all Living Trust that is right for every family, nor one so advanced that even attorneys haven't heard of it. Don't believe everything you hear. Avoiding probate cost should not be your only goal, particularly at the expense of your loved ones. Providing a thoughtful and secure system for distributing your wealth after you are gone is the goal, and that is what makes you the hero. Your estate plan is your last chance to speak.

Will a Revocable Trust Save Money by Avoiding Probate?

Although we have yet to discuss what a "Revocable Trust" actually is, everyone seems to have a preconceived notion of what it can do. It is a fact that a Revocable Trust is not a "Credit Shelter Trust" and it is not designed to help avoid taxes on your property by your heirs, nor is it designed to save money by avoiding probate. What it *is* designed for will be discussed in Chapter Eleven.

A Revocable Trust can help avoid huge potential family and legal problems by avoiding probate, but for most couples or families it does not necessarily save money by the mere fact it avoids probate. Think of it like this: when your spouse or parent dies, there is a lot of work to be done by somebody. This is when you hope the trust has been properly funded and all affairs are in order, or you will end up in probate court anyway.

There will be the funeral, the paperwork to access bank accounts, the safe deposit box (how do you get in?) the location of stocks, bonds, insurance policies, IRAs, retirement and pension funds, the management of these accounts, the paying of bills, conclusion of personal matters, selling of businesses and other real property, dealing with business partners, or those who think they have something coming, and filing personal income tax, inheritance tax and perhaps federal estate tax returns.

Then there will be the process of accounting for personal property and dividing it among heirs, and perhaps the family residence may have to be vacated and sold.

These chores cannot be avoided. Leaving it all for an attorney to do would be expensive. But with the help of a trustee, one who is disentangled from family politics and not subject to unrealistic demands and bias, he or she may be the only person who can get the job done right without the aid of court administration. Once again, choosing the right trustee is an integral part of managing a successful distribution of an estate, and in many cases you are asking a lot.

Are the statutory probate fees, and the combined price of the statutory attorney and executor fees, worth avoiding by drafting a Revocable Trust?

The answer depends on if you believe administration of your estate will need supervision.

When you consider the average estate for the moderately successful Baby Boomer in California is approximately two million dollars, you begin to wonder if these fees are worth it. Afterall, once you are gone, there is nothing more an attorney or executor can do to save the estate money beyond what has already been planned.

On the other hand, if you do not use the services of probate, nobody is supervising whether the job is done right. Unless there is a trustworthy person in control of the money, and savvy in business and personal affairs, there are a lot of well intentioned mistakes that can be made.

Personalities can clash, greed can raise its ugly head, and power can corrupt. Choosing the players in your estate becomes a matter of checks and balances on your priorities. Only you know what is best for your family.

CHAPTER EIGHT

Trustees

The first thing you need in order to create a trust is someone who can serve as trustee. In order for a trust to work, and this means any kind of trust, you need a good trustee. These people are hard to come by. Perhaps even your spouse would not be the best person for the job due to lack of business acumen.

The trustee is expected, above all else, to preserve the capital of the trust account, while at the same time tempering that duty by maintaining the lifestyle of the beneficiaries by the growth of assets. This means the trustee must not only be a prudent investor, but a compassionate friend to those they serve. It is not an easy job and demands a constant balancing act in order to make people happy. Some beneficiaries want their money and they want it now!

Being a trustee puts a man or woman under the highest fiduciary duty imposed by law to service those beneficiaries whom he has the duty to protect, whether it be their financial interest, their physical well being, their education, or any other role that may be part of their directive. It basically boils down to being able to form good judgment amidst the temptation of many wrong options.

For example, a good trustee may be a person who does absolutely nothing with a trust full of solid stocks paying decent dividends even when there are fortunes to be made in the stock market, such as the dot-com business in 2000-2001. The good judgment of the trustee to stick with the blue-chip stocks would make him look like a genius when the dot-com market crashed, all because he had the good judgment to keep his hands off the stock. A trustee also has a duty to diversify assets to minimize risk.

But when it comes to a great example of a trustee, how would you like George Washington to be responsible for carrying out your last wishes? Here is what Thomas Jefferson wrote about Washington's character when it came to good judgment:

"Perhaps the strongest feature in (Washington's) character was prudence, never acting until every circumstance, every consideration, was maturely weighed; refraining if he saw a doubt, but, when once decided, going through with his purpose, whatever obstacle opposed."

Of course, good judgment comes in all colors, as does loyalty and trust. A trustee should be a person familiar with your business, preferably someone who knows you, and who will use this knowledge to make the best decisions for you in the future.

If you do not know a person you can trust in that role, then an attorney whose life and career experience has been a model of fiduciary duty, may merit consideration. Ethically, however, it is not normally regarded to be in the family's best interest to have the attorney who writes the trust also serve as the trustee.

There is also the option of a bank or professional trustee. This may be appropriate for a portion of the larger estate because that is who they are set up to serve (generally appropriate if your assets are in excess of $2 million).

When you choose a trustee you need to take the above mentioned qualities into consideration. Banks often have departments that specialize in managing trust accounts, and professional trustees are well-suited to accept substantial deposits and distribute money by computer according to a directive in your trust. However, that says little for their human qualities.

These institutions normally view trust funds as though the money was bequeathed to them personally, and their actions can be motivated by the fact they are paid a percentage of the gross estate. They intend to keep that gross as high as possible which is encouraged by the law. They have clients with much more money, and no time to care about the little millionaires. They are simply not equipped to handle the day-to-day needs of a person with any compassion.

Therefore, they are not equipped to personally service the "smaller" beneficiary.

This is why allowing someone other than yourself to choose a trustee for your trust "helter skelter," is the wrong way to go about it. I am sure if you are reading this book you have more brains than that. But before you pick a trustee, or request someone to act as trustee, think of what you are asking of them. You are putting them in a position of serious responsibility and perhaps a target for unruly or dissatisfied heirs.

Not only must they manage the "money" you accumulated over your life, but either "may" or "shall" distribute the principle of the trust to beneficiaries. This means they either "shall" distribute the trust funds based on reasonable proof of the beneficiary's needs, putting the beneficiary more in control; or "may" distribute the funds, leaving distribution of the funds up to the trustee's sole discretionary power. Your choice of words here is very important.

These issues of who controls the distribution of trust funds, and by what standard of discretion the trustee may use to distribute those funds, are governed by the language used in the trust. That is why standard "boilerplate" forms are tricky if not fatal if you don't know what you are doing.

In the case of "shall" distribute the funds, here is why the beneficiary is more in control. If the beneficiary does not get the funds they have requested from the trustee, they can sue the trustee and win if they can persuade the judge they have a reasonable need (for say, plastic surgery?). This is because the trustee is under a direct order to release funds in such a situation.

On the other hand, if the trustee "may" distribute the funds, the beneficiary has little control because even if they can show they have a reasonable need, the trustee is under no order to distribute funds to them. Therefore, the judge is less inclined to order the trustee to pay the beneficiary, regardless of their perceived "reasonable need."

It does not take an attorney to see the potential conflict brewing between the trustee and the beneficiary when different priorities collide. The only instructions left to the trustee may be the language in the trust telling them to provide for the beneficiary's "health, support, maintenance and education," or "comfort, welfare and happiness." But what does that mean to the trustee trying to preserve the principal? What does it mean to the beneficiary who wants to take a trip abroad?

Remember, whatever your relationship with the trustee, whether they are a trusted friend, a professional, or a bank, it ends upon your death. The trustee is left to figure out if providing for your children's health includes plastic surgery, or if providing maintenance and support includes buying tools for a mechanic's garage, or art for an art gallery, or instruments for a medical lab.

If it is a "Pot Trust," for every dollar spent on Johnny's musical training at Julliard, there is a dollar taken from Suzie's need for world-wide travel. That can create friction and make the trustee a mark for litigation. The accusations can be a breach of fiduciary duty and abuse or, at the very least, of bad faith.

One of the most important principles of the family dynamic is your presence and relationship with the family members may be the very magic that ensures everybody gets along. Without you, your family is left to their own resolve. This can produce some pretty selfish results, which currently fill the probate courts.

Who Does Your Attorney Represent?

Your estate planning must begin before you meet with an attorney. Upon making an appointment you should be sent a *questionnaire* such as the one that can be found in the Appendix in this book.

The questionnaire in this Appendix is designed for *married persons,* but is easily adaptable for a single person. (A single person's estate is simpler because there are no ownership issues). You should fill out these forms to the best of your ability. As we have discussed, this mental exercise will prepare you for the breadth and scope of estate planning. Even if you only read it, you will better understand the task at hand. But if you are going to do this right, you will not only read it, but sit down with your spouse and envision of what your estate plan will consist.

If you are married, you must determine if an attorney will represent both of you, or just one of you. If you have been married to the same person and share the same children, then the answer may be easy.

But what if:

- Each party wants confidential advice and guidance concerning their separate property;
- It is a recent marriage and one spouse has substantially more than the other;
- Both parties have substantial separate property and need separate planning;
- Each party desires to pass their separate property to different persons;
- One spouse wants to provide for a child from a previous marriage;
- One spouse wants to provide for children from a previous marriage;

- One party has corporate holdings that have been in his or her family for years;
- The attorney also represents business partners in a family business;
- One spouse thinks the other wants to take unfair advantage of them;
- Outside interests are competing to gain favor over each spouse;
- The attorney represents the bank or trust company?

In these situations, it may be necessary for the attorney to have frank discussions with both parties, in private, concerning the desires of the other spouse. This may not be desired by either party, regardless of the fact it would help communication between spouses so there are no misunderstandings, particularly because your attorney wants to draft a trust in your best interest, as a couple.

If there is a conflict between the couple, then it must be pointed out by the attorney, even if you are already aware of it, and you should receive a letter in writing explaining his opinion of what the conflict is. After that, you can determine if you want to go forward with just one attorney. Remember, it is your job and the attorney's liability to write a Revocable Trust that is not disadvantageous to one of the spouses on its face. If it is, the attorney will be held liable unless he has the written permission of the disadvantaged spouse to write the trust as agreed.

It is, therefore, sometimes necessary to bring a second attorney into the planning process so both sides are protected. This extra attorney may be prudent regardless of the fact it could cost twice as much. However, experience has shown most people, regardless of their wealth, are unwilling to bear that cost no matter how smart it is. That is why you and your spouse need to determine your estate plan first, before interviewing an attorney.

Why You Need An Attorney

You need an attorney for liability reasons. Attorneys are supposed to know what they are doing. If they don't, they risk losing their license or being sued for malpractice. That is strong motivation to do a good job. If an attorney holds him or herself out in the field of estate planning, you can safely assume they can handle your job.

That does not apply to hiring an attorney for litigation. In that case, it doesn't matter if the litigation is over a probate matter or any other kind of court battle, the trial attorney operates on a different field of play.

There are many attorneys whose preference is to never go to court, or to do so only for administrative matters. This is not the person you want to hire for a Will contest against your brother to get your mother's house back from his manipulative wife.

Most estate planning issues revolve around a peaceful analysis of what you want to accomplish and how to do it. There is nothing in this book that requires certified specialization for the attorney to apply the general estate planning principles to your life. However, it does mandate the attorney be knowledgeable on the current state of the law. That is a must.

In large part, that is the purpose of this book. The more familiar you are with the concepts and language of the subject, the more accurately you can communicate with an attorney in order to determine if you want to work with them.

Do not be afraid to pay a *minimal* fee for an initial consultation so you can decide if you like one attorney over the other. You can always get recommendations from friends and family. Ask your neighbors and associates at clubs and work. Take it as advice, but make your own decisions. Remember, it all depends on the source.

Your legacy concerns your most important personal matters; act like it. The best approach for hiring an attorney is to make two or three different appointments. But before you arrive for the consultations, have your mind set that you are going to wait and talk to the other attorneys before deciding on which one to hire. If one is so good you do not want to wait, that will be a pleasant surprise and you can sign the engagement letter (contract), after reading it. On the other hand, beware of smooth talkers, which is why you were going to interview several attorneys in the first place. So it is best to wait.

Keep the above routine in perspective. If you know all you want is a Revocable Trust, then there is not much to think about since you have it figured out already. Much has already been said about the nature of the relationship you want with your attorney. Litigation attorneys aside, all the virtues of a Boy Scout are what is best in an attorney...trustworthy, loyal, helpful, friendly, courteous, kind... To that list you want to add extremely knowledgeable and vigilant.

Where do you find such an attorney? You owe it to yourself to make an inquiry to your state's Bar Association to at least make sure the attorney is in good standing, with no disciplinary actions taken against them. Remember, anybody can file a complaint, but if there are any complaints that have been filed you need to investigate. If disciplinary action has been taken, find yourself another attorney.

In California the website is www.Calbar.org.

The Litigation Attorney

Make no mistake about it; you do not want the stress of litigation. As you get older, although there is always something worth fighting over, there is nothing that will shorten your lifespan quicker than litigation. Sitting in a courtroom below the judge, with your brother at the opposite end of the table, and fighting over your mother's family home, is not what you want to do, ever. It is hateful, but sometimes it is also necessary.

On the other hand, things happen. Perhaps during your mother's last couple of months your brother's wife went every day and comforted her through her illness. Perhaps she cooked, cleaned and cared for her. And, as your mother became more ill and the dosages of her medicine became more potent, she came to only recognize your sister-in-law as the person who loved her most.

Unbeknown to you, she had your sister-in-law make an appointment, perhaps at the sister-in-law's suggestion, with your mother's old attorney. On a day she was feeling pretty good she went to the attorney, escorted by her daughter-in-law, and changed her Will so the family home was left to your brother and his wife, and you were left only $25,000, while the home was worth $1 million.

It may come as quite a shock after the funeral when you find out, particularly when the house is worth $1 million, and particularly when you and your brother had previously talked about how you would each receive equal shares. What would you do?

First, you would probably try and talk to your brother, but when he told you to go pound sand, what would you do? Maybe you would go to an attorney and tell him he could use your entire $25,000 inheritance to fight this inequity, you just want your half of the house.

There would be a problem with this arrangement immediately. The Will no doubt would have a "no contest clause" meaning if you contest the Will and lose, you will not be eligible to receive the $25,000 inheritance.

Perhaps you decide to take the risk and put up your own $25,000 to fight the Will. Your attorney advises that you have a pretty good case. Afterall, your mother was very ill at the time, under the influence of drugs, and could have been incompetent to rewrite her Will. Her state of mind would have to be examined. Neighbors and friends would have to be interviewed. Her doctor would have to be deposed, as well as her attorney, the sister-in-law, and of course your brother.

At each one of these depositions, are expensive, you will be in a constant state of anxiety and despair each time someone testifies under oath how sane your mother was until the day of her death. The tension in the room when your brother and his wife are deposed will make you feel sick every time they lie to support their own cause.

But if your attorney is good enough, he will make them feel even worse. Hopefully, their minds will fill with doubt about whether it is worth proceeding. They have to pay for their attorney the same as you, only their desire to win is not fueled by the same desire that burns in you from feeling deceived.

Meanwhile, the attorneys are going to court on a regular basis and fighting over every little thing that surrounds your mother's estate and the need for information. Motions are made to seek and destroy the opposition, while the cost of litigation just keeps going up.

The best you can hope for at this point is that the other side has had enough and will throw in the towel. This is much easier for them to do in a contested Will case because the money was not theirs in the first place. It is much easier to give up something you never had. If their decision is to give you half of the home that was never theirs, then your attorney has done an outstanding job.

If the case goes to trial, it is impossible to say who will win. The arguments are strong on both sides, but in a probate case, the facts are heard and decided upon by a judge, not a jury, unless there are special circumstances. What that judge believes and how he reads the evidence is anybody's guess. That is why you want to stay out of court, and compromise your case by settling for the most you can get. You need only think how terrible it would be to lose, and nobody has the answer to that question before the decision by the court.

CHAPTER NINE

"Credit Shelter Trusts"

Credit Shelter Trust was a subject George Washington need know nothing about even though he was awarded five honorary doctors of law degrees from Harvard (1776), Yale (1781), University of Pennsylvania (1783), Washington College (1789), and Brown (1790). That is because the degrees were accepted by him only to enhance his titles, and there was no such thing as "estate tax" to which a Credit Shelter Trust would apply. Those were the days my friend!

Beginning in 2010, certain estate planning tools will be necessary to create effective estate plans, particularly for the larger estates. After you learn how the tools are implemented and how they work, you cannot help but wonder who created these tools, let alone getting them Congress and into law. These estate planning tools will be necessary to understand in order to get your estate planning job done right.

But before getting into their names, their definition and how they work, it is first necessary to understand the meaning of the difference between tax "avoidance" and tax "evasion." Afterall, tax evasion will get you into the same tight fix it got Al Capone, but tax avoidance is a different matter, and totally legal.

I believe it has never been explained better, in more precise layman's terms than by the great Supreme Court Justice Louis D. Brandeis. This was the type of man who could critically analyze a Credit Shelter Trust at first glance and know if it was used right or wrong. He is what law school professors properly refer to as a legal genius. Here is how Justice Brandeis put it:

> *"Where I live in Alexandria, Virginia, near the Supreme Court building there is a toll bridge across the Potomac River. When in a rush, I pay the toll and get home early. However, I usually drive outside the downtown section of the city, and cross the Potomac on a free bridge. If I went over the toll bridge and through the toll without paying I would be guilty of tax evasion. However, if I go the extra mile and drive outside the city of Washington to the free bridge, I am using a legitimate, logical and suitable method of tax avoidance. And, I am providing a useful social service as well."*

You can mark this Chapter Nine as the halfway point to creating a successful Revocable Trust. Your estate plan should begin to come into focus by learning what tools are at hand to perform a specific purpose.

You can begin by looking at the flow chart vision of the perfect estate plan for the moderately successful baby boomers who perhaps have a son or daughter from a previous marriage, or anybody else they want to make certain is entitled to inherit something upon the death of the surviving spouse. That is the purpose of a QTIP Trust, all of which is discussed in Chapter Eleven under Revocable Trust.

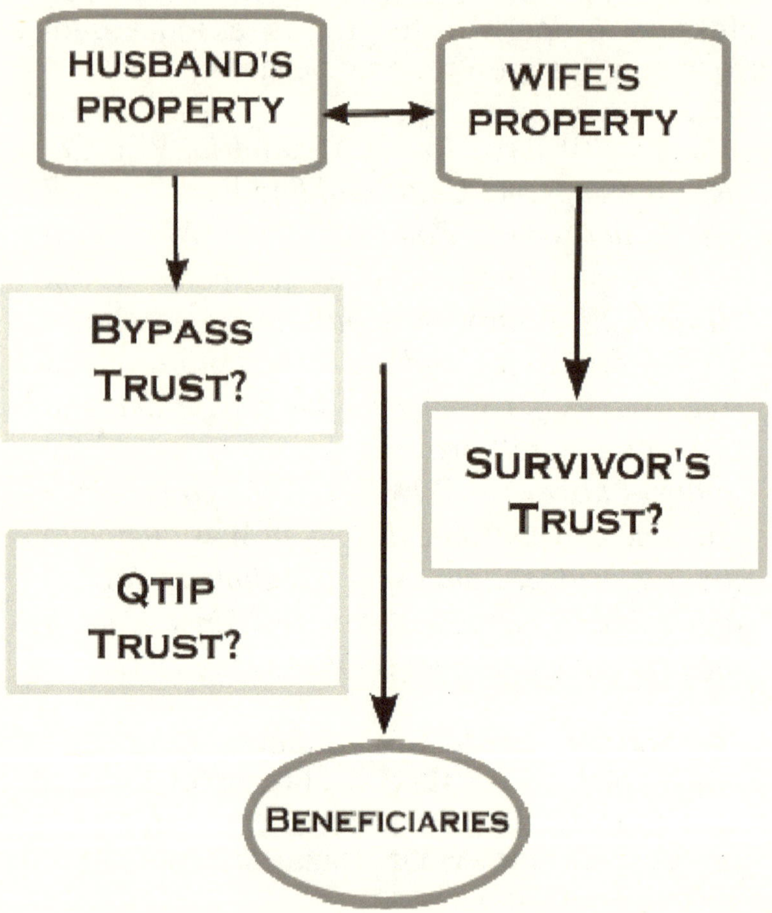

The flow chart above also provides a trust for the assets of the separate and/or one-half the community property of the first spouse to die, to fund the Bypass Trust. $2 million can go into the

Bypass Trust if they die in 2008, or $3.5 million in 2009, and no limit in 2010. The income of this trust will go to the surviving spouse, and maybe to their children, during the lifetime of the surviving spouse. After the death of the surviving spouse, no tax is due on the growth of the Bypass Trust. The children will also not pay taxes on the Survivor's Trust if the surviving spouse also dies in 2008, 2009 or, 2010 because it is less than the exemption amount. That is the purpose of a Bypass Trust, also discussed in Chapter Eleven. But beware, it all changes by 2011.

If only it was that simple.

Conceptually speaking it is that simple. But if you were told by an attorney, or anyone else, that the above flow chart represents the right estate plan for you, it would be the same as accepting the sale's pitch that any boilerplate Revocable Trust is the right one for everyone. (The same as it is for your next-door neighbor – old Fritz, - the one with all the junk in his front yard).

Upon learning about a QTIP Trust, you may decide you do not want one because when the surviving spouse dies, it will be added back on top of their Survivor's Trust. Your children from that marriage, or the one before that, will pay the 45% tax on the "applicable exemption amount" which is the tax exemption for the stated years. You may decide to provide for your child from a previous marriage through a written directive in the Bypass Trust. On the other hand, upon learning how the Bypass Trust works you may not want your wife to be the trustee for various reasons. Clearly, there is no one-size-fits-all flow chart.

Some attorneys make a simple recommendation to couples, with or without children, to put the maximum limit of the anticipated marital tax exemption in the Bypass Trust and leave everything else to the Survivor's Trust. That is hardly a thoughtful suggestion when you do not know what the "marital exemption" means or how a Survivor's Trust works, which is also discussed in Chapter Eleven.

Unfortunately the same trust is called by several different generic names such as what we are calling the Survivor's Trust. It is also known as the Marital Trust, and the same Bypass Trust we are talking about is called a Non-Marital Trust. This sometimes makes it confusing when discussing these trusts with people who call it another name - an old fashioned name. That is why you must know the meaning of the trust and understand how it fits into the estate planning vision.

The trusts may be known by several different names but the names I am providing in this book are the modern, most up to date terms most commonly used today. I know these names, because I attend numerous seminars and have read many, many treatises that explain how the names have changed over the years. This is particularly true with Living Trusts and Revocable Trusts.

However, before you can understand the Credit Shelter Trusts, you must understand the federal marital tax exemption which was introduced in Chapter Seven, under Introducing *the Smaller Estate Plan.*

CHAPTER TEN

How the Federal Exemption Tax Works

There are three main factors that decide how to go about planning for your estate:

1. The size of your family;

2. How much money you want to save them or give them; and

3. The aggregate value of your assets.

The primary purpose for married couples to utilize trusts, beyond the simple avoidance of probate, is to preserve their assets for long term beneficiaries, and to avoid tax payments upon the death of the surviving spouse. That is why you must first complete the steps in the preceding chapters. You must list and value what you own, decide with your spouse, the character of the property, and how the title is held, as well as decide where it is going. This allows you to know where your estate stands in relation to the marital exemption tax.

As far as avoiding taxes upon the death of the first spouse, there is no need to worry about that, except for the fact you missed the opportunity to save taxes through estate planning when your spouse was alive. You can be an eccentric billionaire, leave all of your estate to your surviving spouse, and he or she will not have to pay a single penny of taxes on the inherited money from the first spouse's half of the billion dollars. That is called a "marital tax deduction."

Who pays the estate tax in the marital deduction scenario are the children, beneficiaries, or charities who are to receive the billion dollars after the surviving spouse dies. That could be 55% on everything over a million dollars if they die after 2010. But nobody knows what the new administration will pass as our estate tax law in 2009.

As it stands right now, the only time a billionaire's descendents could really profit is if their benefactors died in the year 2010 because there is no estate tax, which is a horrible thing to wish for. It is hard to believe Congress will not do something about it before 2010 given the state of the economy, and the upcoming 2008 election.

Until 2010 and after, whatever becomes the new estate tax law, the couple who wants to benefit their children, whether they have a billion dollars or $100,000, may want to take advantage of what is called a "marital exemption."

Whether it is a Revocable Trust that funds a "Credit Shelter Trust" after death, or a Last Will and Testament which can do the same, all it takes to frustrate your plan is a disgruntled heir. Good estate planning includes guarding the plan from malicious interlopers, as well as protecting the ones you love. This is why careful thought is so important. As the old saying goes, "To succeed, you must follow the five Ps: previous planning prevents poor performance!"

As an example, consider what would happen if your surviving parent died in 2008, or after 2010, and left you an estate worth $4 million. Your parents could have saved you the sum of $920,000 in taxes in 2008 as long as they had drawn up a Revocable Trust and taken advantage of a "nonmarital tax exemption trust," or what is known as a Bypass Trust. And, if the surviving parent died after 2010, and assuming the tax exemption reverts back to $1 million and your parents did not take advantage of it, it would cost $1.3 million in estate taxes. That would be a real pity.

Tax estate planning is *really* about maximizing the distribution to your heirs and making sure it is distributed to them without the enormous burden of having to sell almost half the estate to pay the taxes. Nobody else can do it for them but you. Would anybody else be to blame for the taxes they pay but you? This is not what heroes are made of.

Here is how the officially named "Federal Exemption Tax" works:

First, you have to be married. Second, your spouse has to be a U.S. citizen. Third, each spouse has an opportunity during their lifetime (not after death) to set aside from their share of the estate, the "federal tax exclusion limit" which in the year 2008 is $2 million. This is $2 million the family does not have to pay estate tax on whenever a single person dies, or the surviving spouse dies.

In the case of the married couple, this "applicable exclusion amount" will never be included as part of the surviving parent's estate, because it will be housed in a safe harbor called a Bypass Trust, if the estate is large enough. The children will not be taxed on the money at the death of their second parent. This is not the case with the QTIP Trust as will be explained.

This means you can put $2 million (your half of a $4 million estate) into a Credit Shelter Trust, such as the Bypass Trust, when you die and this money can be held tax free and be used for the benefit of your surviving spouse during her entire life.

Then, the $2 million, or what is left of it, will pass directly to your children upon the death of the second parent. The children do not pay federal tax on either the $2 million that was in the Bypass Trust, or the $2 million left by the surviving spouse because it is not above the applicable exclusion amount. If this is not done, they would pay $900,000 in additional tax.

It should be noted again there is also a "marital tax deduction," which is the alternative to the tax exemption. This deduction allows a husband (or wife), as stated above, to leave their spouse any amount of money they want, even $1 billion dollars upon their death, and the surviving spouse will not have to pay any tax on it. They could use the entire amount to support any kind of extravagant lifestyle they preferred.

However, if they died in 2008, any amount of that $1 billion left over in the estate will be taxed at 45% on all portions over the $2 million exemption. That is exactly why a Bypass Trust is so beneficial. It allows a larger amount of your estate's value to transfer "tax free" to the beneficiaries.

The table below shows how legislators gradually raised this tax exempt amount for each spouse's estate beginning in 2001: from $675,000 in 2001 to $2 million in 2006 to 2008.

The column at the right shows the highest tax bracket for each year at which an estate may be taxed on all sums above the exempt amount, and unlimited in 2010. In 2001 it was 55% on amounts over $675,000, and in 2006, any amount over $2 million was taxed at 46%, etc.

YEAR	AMOUNT EXEMPT FROM ESTATE TAX	HIGHEST TAX BRACKET
2001	**$675,000**	**55%**
2002	**$1,000,000**	**50%**
2003	**$1,000,000**	**49%**
2004	**$1,500,000**	**48%**
2005	**$1,500,000**	**47%**
2006	**$2,000,000**	**46%**
2007	**$2,000,000**	**45%**
2008	**$2,000,000**	**45%**
2009	**$3,500,000**	**45%**
2010	**Unlimited**	**N/A**
2011	Must wait to see what legislators enact.	

Again, each spouse has the opportunity to set aside the "nonmarital tax exempt amount" of their estate value before they die. In 2008, a husband can put $2 million into a trust from his estate for the benefit of his wife, and ultimately for his children, without them having to pay a penny of tax when their mother dies. Of course, that is only fair since the earned income has already been taxed by the government! But it may also include highly appreciated assets.

More importantly, if the husband (it is always easier to assume the husband will die first because statistically it is true and it makes examples easier) fails to exclude this amount from his estate by setting it aside in a trust, he forfeits the right to exclude the applicable amount and it will be taxed after the death of his surviving wife. If she dies in 2008 the heirs will have to pay $900,000 in taxes on the other $2 million.

Also, keep in mind that the estate tax, above, and the federal gift tax, are a "unified" tax exemption, not "in addition to" exemptions. This means if you gift a million dollars to your children over your life, you have only one million left to use as the marital deduction.

In 2002, the gift tax exemption was raised to $1 million. The estate tax and gift tax are mutually inclusive in that they draw from the same exemption pot, the federal exemption tax.

Therefore, if you give $1 million in gifts (in addition to the annual exclusion amount that was raised to $12,000 in 2006) it is subtracted from the estate tax exemption when you die. ($2 million in 2008 minus the $1 million gift tax exclusion leaves $1 million still to be used as an estate tax exemption.)

Nobody knows for certain what will happen when the federal exemption tax is repealed in 2010, but if Congress does nothing new to alter what is already in place, the exemption is scheduled to revert to $1 million and the tax will increase up to 55%. It is unclear what will really happen. That is because there is this big thing in the way called the 2008 presidential election.

If the marital exemption does revert to $1 million in 2011, as the sunset clause is presently written, that makes learning how to use the "Credit Shelter Trusts" much more necessary for millions of people than if the exemption tax was frozen at $5 million, as was proposed in 2007 before the Senate, but did not pass.

The History of Estate Tax

Here is a short history on the estate tax and how it began. It was not always the law of the land. Congress first proposed such a law in 1787 in order to raise funds for building the American Navy, but it was a far cry from the tax we have today. A decedent's real estate was not even brought into it. It was based on personal property and was so small it was more like a contribution than a tax.

During most of the nineteenth century there was no inheritance tax except for three years before the end of the Civil War, after which it was repealed, and again in 1898 to raise funds for the Spanish/American War. It was also repealed after that war, and like the two previous inheritance taxes it did not include real estate. So you can see, the idea of repealing the "death tax" may not be as radical as you imagined.

Much of people's acceptance of this tax today is because it came back to life in 1916 before WWI, only this time it never left. Today's generations accept it as just another tax. Much of this is based on such idioms as that of Benjamin Franklin, who stated categorically the only two things you can't avoid are "death and taxes." But that was Ben Franklin talking; it was the United States Congress who conceived taxing your death and passing the tax on to your children to pay from your estate, even though you had already paid taxes on that same earned income and the properties you worked your whole life to accumulate.

The estate tax, as we know it today, was first passed in 1916 in anticipation of arming for WWI. When the tax was challenged as unconstitutional in the courts under *New York Trust v. Eisner* (1921), it was held by the Supreme Court that the tax was *"fair because it only reached the property of the decedent and the tax was easily avoided by taxpayers who could afford to make lifetime gifts."* In other words, it was totally acceptable according to the Supreme Court for the rich to not pay the tax as long as they were rich enough to make lifetime gifts. **Today these are called "Credit Shelter Trusts" and you do not have to be rich to use them, but you do have to use them before you die.**

For some reason, unlike the other inheritance taxes, this estate tax was not repealed after the war was over and has gone through an amalgamation of changes for various reasons ever since. The most constant purpose appears to be to break up the large concentration of wealth coveted by the ultra-wealthy.

In 1981, 27 years ago, the "death tax" deduction was at the dramatic low of $60,000. After President Reagan was elected in 1980, the estate tax exemption was raised tenfold from $60,000 to $600,000, at a 55% tax rate on anything over $600,000. Can you imagine going back to that rate now?

It was not until President Bush was elected in 2000 that he managed to get the "Estate Tax Reformation Act," which had lingered unsuccessfully the year before, passed through a majority of Republican congressmen and senators. That tax bill had been vetoed by President Clinton. The official name of the tax bill we are taxed by today is called the "Economic Growth and Taxpayer Reconciliation Tax of 2001."

This is the most important thing you need to know in order to understand the entire death and inheritance system and how to avoid or defer paying those estate taxes.

Notice I said avoid or defer. I did not say evade paying the taxes because that would be illegal. The government gives you the ability to create a "Credit Shelter Trusts" to help you avoid paying the taxes; it does not give you anything to help you evade them. There is a great quote by former Supreme Court Justice Louis Brandeis on page 99. Justice Brandeis is a man revered by all legal scholars and he perfectly explains the distinct difference between avoiding taxes and evading taxes.

According to the "reconciliation act" in 2008 each spouse is allowed $2 million should you happen to die before the end of the year. And in 2009, it goes up to $3.5 million, and in 2010 the exemption is unlimited. So that is a good year to die if you have lots and lots of money, or so your heirs think. Unfortunately, although not etched in stone, the new administration is just not going to let that happen. In all likelihood a new tax bill will be passed prior to 2010. The prediction is the new exemption will be frozen at between $1 million and $3.5 million, at 50% or 55% tax. But as far as estate planning goes there is no bigger issue than this one for the 2008 election.

To think of a middle-class family worth $5 million as being part of the "ultra rich" simply defies the American dream. In 2006 when the question of repealing the estate tax (and the Republicans were three votes short with McCain's absence), Senate Minority Leader Harry M. Reid (D-Nev.) who led the opposition to the tax measure stated that "under the bill, 8,100 of the wealthy and well-off hit the jackpot, while millions of working families get $8,000 billion in (federal) debt." The "wealthy and well off" hit the jackpot?

When Senator Reid is talking about 8,100 Americans as "wealthy and well off," he can only be talking about people who have hundreds of millions of dollars, if not billions. These people are not going to pay any estate taxes regardless of the law even if they have to leave the country and take all those billions of dollars in capital with them, which nobody wants, and Congress fully understands. There are approximately 300 million people in America and if 8,100 (that's .000027% of the population) hit the jackpot, so be it.

At the same time, 2,991,900 citizens are hitting the jackpot also by not having to worry about how to handle the death tax to pay for Iraq, the securities and mortgage home bailouts, the strangle-hold on gasoline prices, and the latest death grip on the American motor companies and airlines. With the repeal of the death tax the non-ultra rich families can pass on their family farms and businesses and college educations to their children or charities, which are what they have been working for anyway. What else would we be more concerned about then the heritage of our families?

The counter argument to this is that even if we left the tax exemption at the 2008 value of $2 million, an American would have a higher chance of dying by falling off a roof, than having to pay taxes on their estate when they die because so few citizens have a gross value in their estate of $4 million, or $2 million per spouse, or individual.

Does this group of Middle Americans need to be protected? These are the ones who do not have the common sense to take estate planning seriously because they came from a background of middle class values where their parents never made that kind of money. They do not do what is explained in this book. As it has been reiterated many times in this book, too many things can go wrong during the administration of the estate after the first to die is gone. It only takes one disgruntled heir to land you back in probate court where the judge may not see things the way these sophisticated laws were written, or intended.

All that legal cost and stress to your heirs after you are gone is more money than it is worth, particularly to your children. Pay the money now to make sure your estate plan is discussed with a qualified attorney to assure it is right. Even if you are the type who demeans the legal profession by telling lawyer jokes, then have an attorney write your documents for you, and be sure he or she has malpractice insurance. In either case, you are guaranteed a valid estate plan, and you will not feel foolish.

With that being said, a compromise using the 2009 tax-exemption of $3.5 million per spouse may be sufficient to allow a less than ultra-wealthy family to ascend to greater wealth. This can become taxable to help fill the nation's coffers if in Congress's infinite wisdom they deem it necessary in the future. At least, that is a great idea unless you are worth $7 million or more.

A family with $50 million will always find a safe harbor for their wealth in various trusts and corporations. Since most of this money has already been taxed once anyway, why not leave it alone?

There are many countries who have repealed their inheritance tax because they found it only makes the ultra-rich richer. For the middle class, it takes the money they earned with sweat on every dollar, out of their children's hands. These children are America's life blood, with the capitalistic spirit and entrepreneurial DNA it takes to keep this country out of the hands of royalty. The new upper middle class, those with estates worth 1 million to $10 million, includes 8.4 million households today.

(However, an interesting argument against allowing inheritance for any children is that "by abolishing inheritance, all babies would be born equal." I wonder if the prognosticator of that argument has thought through its affect on a provider's will to work.)

At any rate, the next chance for Congress to make a pivotal estate tax decision will be put off until after the election of 2008, since the Democrats turned down an offer to raise the minimum wage, in exchange to freeze the tax exemption at $5 million on March 12, 2008. Whatever the case, it makes it hard to anticipate planning for the future. But rest assured, the estate tax law will be revised before 2010, and there will be no jackpot for anyone.

As for state inheritance tax, this is a state by state proposition. In California, the death tax was eliminated from the state's taxing system by voters in a general election. California will never have an estate "death tax" unless voters decide to vote it back in.

One Creative Option

There is one creative option that would change the entire system. Many professionals believe **the capital gains tax will replace the estate tax**. This means the $200,000 cost basis (original payment for stocks or real estate) on your $500,000 house will "carryover" to the heirs who inherit your house, and not "step up" to the fair market value as is the law presently.

As the law stands now, the house's value is reappraised at death and its cost basis is "stepped up" to fair market value at the time of death when the second parent dies. If your children sell the house when you die, they pay no capital gains tax if the house has not increased in value since your death.

But according to this new capital gains plan, if it is utilized in 2011, the house's original $200,000 value will not "step up" in value at the surviving spouse's death to its $500,000 present market value. What children inherit is the $200,000 cost basis. If they sell the house they pay federal capital gains taxes on the fair market value of the house at 15% federally, and state capital gains tax, which in California is 9.3%. This is a total of approximately 24% tax on the additional $300,000 fair market value of the house. That would be $72,000 in capital gains taxes.

In this case the resulting tax may be inescapable using traditional conservative Credit Shelter Trust and cause parents to gamble on something like a Qualified Personal Residence Trust (QPRT) where the IRS allows you to bet you will outlive their actuary tables. If you do outlive their tables, you get a great tax break determined by how old you are when you entered the trust.

But a QPRT is irrevocable, so if you outlive the actuary tables, you could find yourself homeless, unless you totally trust your kind-hearted children, because the house now belongs to them. Do not worry, there are plenty of options we will discuss in the next chapter.

CHAPTER ELEVEN

The Revocable Trust

Do not think for a second that because you are single you have no need for a Revocable Trust, or that the marital tax exemption does not include you. You may not be married, but the exemption still applies to you. Your rights are the same as the surviving spouse, and in 2008 that is a $2 million exemption.

If you are widowed, or perhaps never got married, you have still had a lifetime of achievement and accumulated the same taxable property as everybody else. No doubt there is a host of nieces and nephews, or even one niece and/or a cousin, or certainly a charity who you would like to bequeath a gift.

I had a client who had seven nieces and nephews for whom she wanted to provide a share of her million dollars in stocks, but only if it was used specifically for their education. She came to my office believing she wanted to set up seven different trusts. But when she learned the impracticality of doing such a thing because of the lack of able and willing family trustees, she chose to open up seven different "529 Plans" under California's system for providing future college funds for everyone at the time they chose to educate themselves.. There is such a program in every state and will be discussed when planning larger estates. Every state has a similar plan.

As stated, the way of keeping your estate from going to the government is accomplished by using various "Credit Shelter Trusts." These trusts shift the tax burden so it does not fall on your children after your death or the death of your spouse.

The popular trend in estate planning is to avoid probate costs and attorney's fees by using a "Living Trust," regardless of practicality. A Living Trust is not a "tax shelter trust" and is not always the right thing to do. An individual's motivation to avoid "probate" often clouds the fact that for a trust to work you first need someone you can have confidence and faith in, no matter what circumstances may arise when you are gone.

That person who has your complete confidence and faith is called a "trustee." For now, think of the trustee as the one person you chose to carry out your wishes, run your business, look out for your children, sell your properties, manage your investments, provide and protect your family, and feed your dog.

Another important aspect of estate planning is to provide a manageable and understandable design of your assets so your chosen trustee can manage your affairs in the event you can no longer do it yourself. Believe it or not, you could become incapacitated due to an accident or incompetent due to health complications.

A Revocable Trust is a written document, similar to a set of rules that explains how your estate will be managed. It becomes immediately effective when you execute the document during your lifetime, rather than after you die like with a Will, and is therefore now popularly called a "living" or "inter vivos" trust.

The trust document creates a legal entity such as the "Jones Trust" that can own real property, businesses, cars, and any other type of asset which can be distributed to you and loved ones both during your life and after.

The rules of the trust can be changed at any time during your life, or completely revoked at any time. Therefore, it is a "revocable" trust. It is properly named an "inter vivos revocable trust." Attorneys like to call it a "Revocable Trust" and most people call it a "Living Trust."

It is also important to understand that although a Revocable Trust avoids probate, it does ***not*** avoid taxes. It can be structured to be a first step to avoiding or deferring taxes, but it has no tax advantage over a Will. That is not the purpose of a Revocable Trust. The types of trusts used to avoid taxes are much more complicated.

Dying Intestate

Of course there can be drastic consequences if you die without a Revocable Trust or a Will leaving your estate to be distributed according to the rules of "Intestate Succession."

Dying without a Will is not necessarily a bad thing if it turns out the way you would have planned it. But as shown earlier in this book, the California laws, followed as the public policy of the majority in all states, shows that the person who dies without a Will or Revocable Trust, faces laws which heavily favor the surviving spouse or children. This is done to the exclusion of the children from a previous marriage.

Besides that scenario, intestate succession can work out exactly the opposite of your desires if you did not want your wife's family to obtain all your separate property. If your wife dies soon after you, your property will be split between her parents, her brothers and sisters or her children from a previous marriage. As you read the chart below to see how intestate succession works, think of an example where there is a bachelor with no children from a previous marriage, and whose parents have predeceased him.

Suppose this lonely bachelor left a Will leaving his entire $2 million estate to the California Hemp Society. When the bachelor's very poor brother and sister find his Will while rummaging through his house after his death, what might they be tempted to do with the Will? This is a question for Angela Lansbury! But with no Will or Trust, the bachelor dies intestate. Since his parents predeceased him, his brother and sister are next in line according to the law in almost every state.

The example below shows that if you die "intestate" your money and property will be divided up along your bloodline, according to many variations of family members' rights, and according to different states. Regardless of what state you reside in there are rules for distribution to your heirs called the "Rules of Intestate Succession." That is your estate plan if you do not plan one yourself. Below is the chart that explains the distribution laws for the State of California. Look under "intestate succession" on the internet for your own state to see if there is any difference.

California's Intestate Succession Chart For Married And Unmarried Decedent	
If you are survived by a:	**Distribution (after court costs, creditors, lawyers, and specific gifts)**
Spouse and child; or more than one child	Surviving spouse is entitled to all the community property and half of decedent's separate property. The other half of the separate property goes to their child at age 18; if more than one child the surviving spouse takes 1/3 of the separate property and 2/3 is shared by the children equally. (If child has died their share goes to their son or daughter)
Spouse, and a child by previous marriage.	Same as above. The surviving spouse takes all community and half the separate property, and other half of separate property goes to child of previous marriage. If more than one child, spouse takes 1/3 and children share 2/3 of separate property equally.
Spouse and a parent or parents, but no child	If the decedent has no living child, and no grandchildren, then spouse takes all community and half the separate property, and the other half goes to decedent's parent, if only one is alive. If both are alive they take 2/3 of separate property.
Spouse and no child, grand child or parent, but sister and half brother	When all lineal descendants are deceased then half of separate property goes to spouse and other half is shared between half and full brothers and sisters, equally.
Child only; or Spouse only	If surviving child only, the child takes all. If surviving Spouse only, spouse takes all.
Not married and no children	All to parents or surviving children of parents (brothers and sisters and/or their surviving issue) if parents are not alive.
None of the above	All to grandparents or surviving children of grandparents (cousins and surviving children of deceased cousins)
No relatives	State of California

You still may be a millionaire!

To dramatize the dream that some people fantasize about, here is how you might be an heir to millions of dollars and not even know it. It is a familiar story about a rich "uncle" somewhere. Although the above chart applies to most family situations, there is always the chance you could still inherit millions of dollars from that rich tycoon you never heard of before:

Suppose the tycoon was married once in his youth, but his wife predeceased him and he died an unmarried man with no children.

Then assume the tycoon's parents had also predeceased him and he was an only child. Assume further that his grandparents are also dead and there are no living aunts or uncles or cousins who are descendents of those grandparents.

Now assume that the former predeceased wife's parents, from long ago, are no longer alive and there are no other descendents of those parents such as a brother-in-law or sister-in-law to the tycoon, or their children who are still alive.

Now assume the tycoon has no next of kin of any kind who can be found, and you are the nearest relative, such as a third cousin by marriage, of the predeceased wife who died forty years ago .... and *Voila, y*ou are the lucky heir to the millionaire tycoon's rich legacy.

The Nuts and Bolts of the Revocable Trusts

There are three good reasons to use a Revocable Trust instead of a Will.

1. It avoids probate and maintains privacy.

2. It allows for easy management of assets if you are disabled and when you die.

3. It is the perfect segue into the Survivor's, Bypass, and QTIP Trusts, as described below.

A Revocable Trust provides the same function as a Will in that it distributes property to your heirs upon death. But in addition to avoiding the cost of probate administration, there are other headaches it helps you avoid.

The trustee of the Revocable Trust can act more quickly to administer and distribute the estate without being bogged down by court supervision. With a Will, the executor can do nothing more than hire a lawyer without the court's further permission.

But to get that permission, the attorney must file a petition to administer the Will, then a petition to confirm sales of property, petitions for instructions, petitions for "almost final distribution," then one for final distribution, and on and on it goes until typically a California probate can last at least one to two years. A typical Revocable Trust can be administered in three to six months, or perhaps longer depending on its complexity regarding the formation of trusts.

Furthermore, this Revocable Trust provides long-term continuity of management of a couple's estate without being interrupted by their death or incapacity by having to wait for the court's permission. An attorney cannot simply walk into court and nonchalantly ask the judge for permission. He has filing requirements of fifteen or thirty days. He must go to court and sometimes wait for hours before his case is called. Then the judge may not be able to decide without a hearing if the permission requested is contested by another heir, and that takes witnesses to testify along with depositions and scheduling along with the court's calendar. Before you know it, a year has gone by and still no decision from the judge has been made. That's how the attorney makes his money, and the headache is well earned.

It must be remembered, there is no functional trust without a husband and wife transferring legal title of their assets into the trust (same with an individual). This demands time and expense to re-title the property and transfer it into the name of the Revocable Trust. Every Baby Boomer, their parents or their children, must re-title ownership of their properties into the name of the trust, such as the "Ben and Kitty

Cartwright Revocable Trust" with Ben and Kitty as Trustees.

Likewise, they must do the same with all the personal tangible property they have listed and talked honestly about as to who owns what and to whom it is suppose to go. This would include farm animals and pets, equipment, or gold coins and watches, as well as cars or an arsenal of weaponry. This could be accomplished with a "Bill of Sale" or an "Assignment of Personal Property" identifying all this individual property being delivered to the trustees of the Revocable Trust. If you wanted to do it like George Washington, you would add a comment as to the significance, or use of each piece of equipment or jewelry, or the custom and manner of how the dog is to be cared. (A pet trust is allowed by law in California as discussed in Chapter Eighteen)

Putting George Washington's virtues aside, it is sometimes fun to jump into a fantasy family American Baby Boomers are familiar with, and most strikingly exhibits the modern day "blended family." It was a TV show watched every Sunday in the sixties, and involved a virtuous father living on a ranch with three sons, all from different mothers who had died from unknown causes. One day a pretty young woman came into town and Ben Cartwright decided to marry her and live out their lives on the Ponderosa.

This gives us the perfect scenario for what could be considered the nuts and bolts of a typical Revocable Trust.

Leaving It All to the New Wife

But before we get to that, we should first discuss the issue of older men marrying a younger woman, and the typical results.

One thing any experienced estate planner will attest to is the common phenomena of the man whose wife dies after thirty years of marriage. Let's call them Mark and Joan. Mark, in due course, then marries a younger woman. The children of the first marriage are grown and have moved out of the house, or perhaps to another state.

In a majority of cases, if there is no plan in place at the time Joan dies, Mark will scrap any notion of leaving both their separate and community property to the adult children, and will inevitably leave it all to the new wife. **It happens all the time.** The children, he feels, are old enough to take care of themselves and his loyalty is to the woman who was with him at the end.

You can be certain this was not Mark and Joan's intent while they were married and in their discussions about their property before she died. But failure to do anything about it makes it a moot question afterward. This situation can be avoided with a Bypass Trust, and preferably a QTIP Trust.

The quest to make certain your children are provided with an inheritance is accomplished by implementing an irrevocable trust which is automatically created at the time of the first spouse's (Joan's) death. This would have prevented the initial plan from being forgotten, or would have given Mark an easy way out. Mark would have received the benefit of all Joan's separate and community property during the course of his life, but upon his death, Joan's property in the trust would be distributed to their children, not to the new wife.

Of course, alternatively, Mark could draw up a Will while married to his new wife and still give the property to the adult children, but this would be a difficult task to perform with his new wife looking over his shoulder and wondering about her security. This is another common reason for precaution, as far as the children from the previous wife go.

The "Typical Revocable Trust"

Getting back to the fantasy couple, there is a diagram of a stereotypical Revocable Trust where the husband dies first, and between the years 2006-2008 when the marital tax deduction is $2 million per spouse.

Using the Cartwright family as our "typical family" may not seem typical to you. But it is estimated at least 60% of American families are blended families. Even George Washington came from a blended family. Washington's father died when he was only eleven years old and he was the son of his father's second wife. George did not inherit Mt. Vernon outright. He first purchased all the land around it before it was left to his older half-brother, Lawrence. George inherited it when his half-brother's widow died.

At eleven years old, George was left with a mother, three younger brothers, and a sister. He left home as a surveyor's assistant at age sixteen. At the age of 28 years, and no doubt motivated by the fact he married Martha Custis, known to be the wealthiest widow in Virginia, if not the entire Colonies, he lusted for land acquisitions and was very astute in his methods of obtaining them.

This included not only vast tracts of land in the West awarded to him for military campaigns before the Revolutionary War, but he was also able to take advantage of neighboring farmers near the Mt. Vernon Estate who inevitably ran into financial difficulties, allowing Mt. Vernon to grow from 2,000 to 8,000 acres, as one by one the neighbors fell on hard times.

At only 26, Martha Custis, came into Washington's life with a daughter and son, and had full authority over the massive estate of her former husband. And though George went childless with Martha himself, all his fortune went to Martha, "for the term of her life," and then to others. Martha's two children (two died out of the four she birthed with her first husband) had died before George: Patsy as a teenager at Mt. Vernon, and John from disease while in the army in 1781 (but not before he sired five children with his wife.) So blended families are not new to America, but what is new is the concept of "Leave it to Beaver" families that grew out of the fifties.

As for the Cartwrights, what is right for Ben and Kitty may not be right for you and your spouse at all. But the sum of the parts illustrates the best tools that work for 90% of American families. Some of the estate planning decisions Ben Cartwright makes may be considered foolish by some, while others would consider them generous. But for educational purposes, the following should help point out why one estate plan does not fit all.

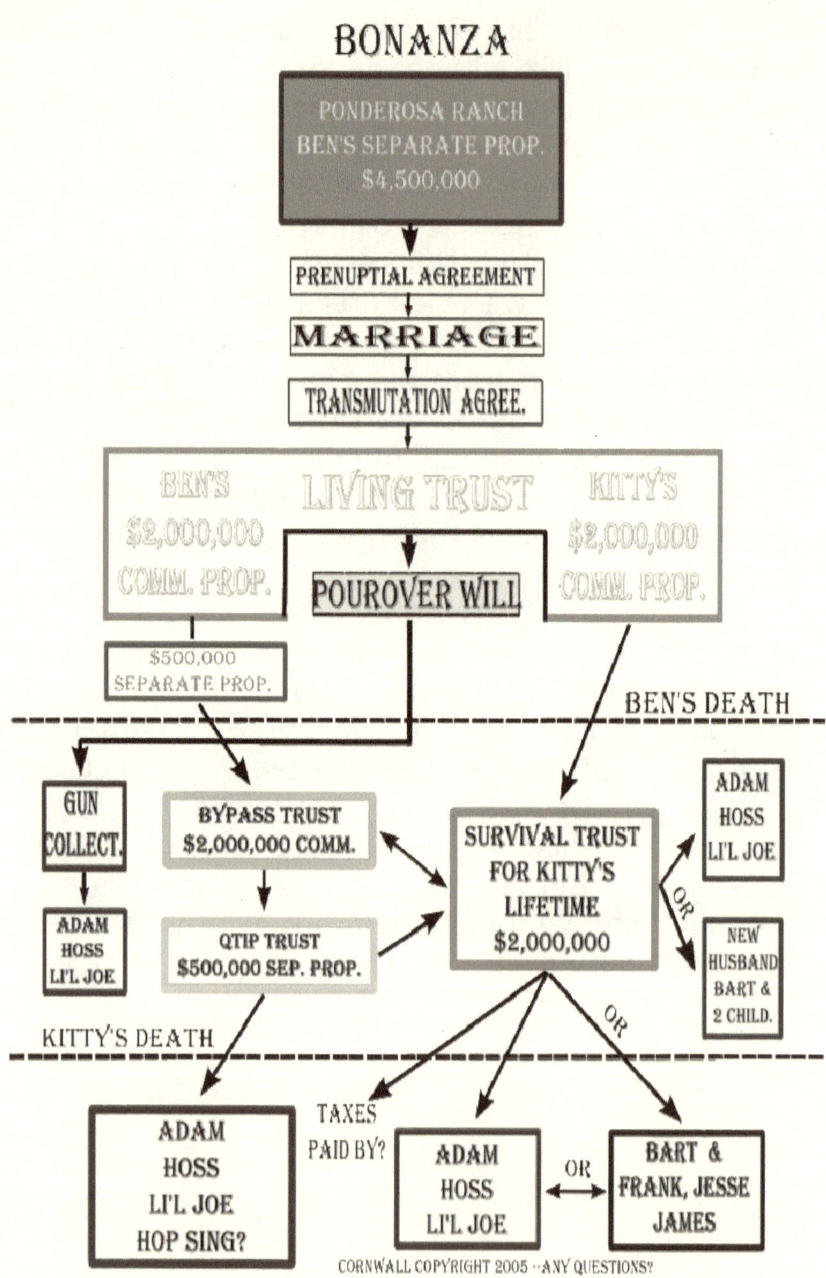

BONANZA
PONDEROSA RANCH
BEN'S SEPARATE PROP.
$4,500,000
PRENUPTIAL AGREEMENT
MARRIAGE
TRANSMUTATION AGREE.
BEN'S
$2,000,000
COMM. PROP.
LIVING TRUST
KITTY'S
$2,000,000
COMM. PROP.
POUROVER WILL
$500,000
SEPARATE PROP.
BEN'S DEATH
GUN
COLLECT.
ADAM
HOSS
LI'L JOE
BYPASS TRUST
$2,000,000 COMM.
QTIP TRUST
$500,000 SEP. PROP.
SURVIVAL TRUST
FOR KITTY'S
LIFETIME
$2,000,000
ADAM
HOSS
LI'L JOE
OR
NEW
HUSBAND
BART &
2 CHILD.
KITTY'S DEATH
OR
ADAM
HOSS
LI'L JOE
HOP SING?
TAXES
PAID BY?
ADAM
HOSS
LI'L JOE
OR
BART &
FRANK, JESSE
JAMES
CORNWALL COPYRIGHT 2005 --ANY QUESTIONS?

This chart is a little beyond the scope of what we have discussed thus far because it includes prenuptial and transmutation agreements. These will be covered in more detail in the chapter illustrating "When Death and Divorce Cause a Transmutational Wreck." But if you follow how the boxes flow by following one pointer to the next and the next, you can begin to see their vision, and how it may be undone by her marriage to another man after Ben dies. It should serve as a prototype, and can be retooled for anybody's estate.

Other flow charts to fit more conventional and unconventional families will be used once the terms of this chart are understood.

As you examine this chart and begin to understand what Ben and Kitty have planned for themselves, the following questions begin to arise:

- Wouldn't Ben want to leave money to his sons outright upon his death?
- Aren't the boys too old to wait for their inheritance until after Kitty dies?
- Couldn't Ben somehow secure the Ponderosa for his sons?
- Why would Ben give so much of his separate property to Kitty?

- Can't Kitty be stopped from taking more than her share from the Bypass Trust and giving her estate to her new husband?

- Did Kitty actually remarry and sire two boys named Frank and Jesse James?

- What about Hop Sing?

These are the types of questions that frequently come too late. The purpose of understanding estate planning is to ask the questions beforehand, while there is still time to do something about it; or make certain the plan delivers exactly the desired outcome.

Here are some oversimplified definitions of the typical Revocable Trust tools used by Ben and Kitty:

Prenuptial Agreement

In an ideal attorney's world all couples, prior to marriage, would sit down and begin preparing for their divorce. They would each put their separate property in a "separate property trust." In this fashion it would be difficult for them to commingle their funds without intentionally doing so, and if they do not commingle, it is not community property, nor is there a need for it to be traced back in case of divorce.

A separate property trust would be a great property identifier and a much cleaner machine than a "premarital contractual agreement" (aka "prenuptial agreement").

A prenuptial agreement is a contract between the bride and groom who determine how their property will be characterized after they are married. It is also good evidence to show the parties' clear intentions at a later date.

But as with any property agreement between spouses, it must honestly address issues about money and what happens upon death. A "prenup" works particularly well when one spouse owns a closely held business corporation, or where a younger man marries an older woman, or where there are children from a previous marriage.

We have already discussed the transmutation agreement in Chapter Four along with how it can save a couple BIG money when the first spouse dies, and the title to the house has been changed from joint tenancy to community property. We have also discussed what would happen if the couple divorced after the transmutation of the property. To find out what happens when death and divorce collide, read Chapter Eighteen.

Pourover Wills

Every Revocable Trust needs to have a Pourover Will. A Pourover Will not only reiterates the last testament of the decedent, but works to "pour" assets into the Revocable Trust, if they had not already been transferred to the trust prior to the death of the first spouse.

This would be the case if Ben Cartwright failed to transfer ownership of his gun collection into the trust before he died. The Pourover Will allows the gun collection to pour into the trust (or it will have to go through probate if its value is over $100,000 in California). It can then be distributed to the children, Adam, Hoss and Little Joe in accordance with the provisions of the Revocable Trust.

The same goes for the ownership of newly acquired property, such as Ben's last acquisition known as the "South Forty." If it was never transferred into the Revocable Trust by Ben, then his executor of the Pourover Will, which would be his oldest son Adam, would do the job upon Ben's death. The property could then be distributed to Kitty and/or the three boys in accordance with the Revocable Trust; perhaps placed in the Bypass Trust or the QTIP Trust.

The downside is if the "South Forty" and/or the gun collection have a value of more than $100,000, then probate will be necessary to transfer the assets into the trust. This is another good reason to update your Revocable Trust every so often. It makes certain new acquisitions have been properly funded into the trust.

Survivor's Trust

Once the Revocable Trust comes to an end at Ben's death, (again, this is a stereotypical example where the man dies first), it typically directs the trustee to create two separate trusts. In our example Ben has died first and his half of the $4 million of community property is going into the Bypass Trust discussed below.

The other half of the estate, since Ben has "transmuted" his separate property into community property, goes into Kitty's Survivor's Trust.

Acting as her own trustee over the Survivor's Trust, is just like being trustee over your Revocable Trust. Kitty has complete control over the property in the Survivor's Trust, and the trust property avoids probate just like in a Revocable Trust. The Survivor's Trust is administered for the sole benefit of Kitty, and by Kitty, and she is entitled to every bit of the monetary distribution of its principal and income for life. She can choose to share the income of this trust with the three boys, or not.

The Survivor's Trust is also revocable at any time, meaning she can do whatever she wants with it. And, because she also retains the "power of appointment" over the trust property, she can leave whatever is left in the trust after she dies to whomever she wants. It does not have to go to Adam, Hoss, or Little Joe, as is the case in the Bypass and QTIP Trusts discussed below.

Also, in this scenario of a $4 million community estate (excluding Ben's separate property), there will be no tax payable upon the death of either spouse because neither of their trusts will be more than the $2 million federal tax exemption allowed in 2008.

Bypass Trust

The Bypass Trust is also known as the "exemption trust" or the "B trust" or the "family trust" or the "Credit Shelter Trust" or the "nonmarital trust," as well as other names. Do not let this confuse you because there is no need for it. It is other people who get the A Trust and the B Trust mixed up. It can be remembered by A, "above" ground like the Survivor's Trust, and B, "below" ground like the Bypass Trust.

All of these names refer to the same trust used to save money from federal estate taxes by properly utilizing the "applicable exemption amount" of the nonmarital tax exemption, which in this case is $2 million. It is now called nonmarital because it goes in the Bypass Trust. What goes in the marital tax exemption goes into the Survivor's Trust. This exemption will most likely revert back to $1 million in 2010, so it is almost too late for the majority us to think about the $2 million exemption, or the $3.5 million exemption next year.

If any spouse puts his $2 million share of the estate (called a "nonmarital tax exemption") into a Bypass Trust for the surviving spouse's benefit during her lifetime, the surviving spouse will not be taxed on that $2 million at 45% if she dies in the year 2008.

What is left of the $2 million in the Bypass Trust (called the "remainder") will go to the spouses' children when the second spouse dies, or to some other heir who both the husband and wife agreed upon when they entered into their Revocable Trust.

For example, in the Cartwright's estate plan the "Bypass Trust" is used as a standard planning tool to make Ben's half of the community property assets available for Kitty's use for her lifetime. However, none of the remaining assets in the Bypass Trust will be added to the gross value of Kitty's estate when she dies. This saves tens of thousands of dollars in estate taxes, as you know from reading "How The Federal Exemption Tax Works" and studying the chart. Ben's Bypass Trust will "bypass" Kitty's estate and be handled separately, unlike the QTIP Trust.

Assuming Ben and Kitty each have a $2 million interest in the $4 million portion of the Bonanza estate, Kitty's half can save $900,000 in taxes by not including Ben's half if she dies in 2008. If Ben does **not** put his share into the Bypass Trust, his $2 million will be added to Kitty's now $4 million estate, and her estate will be taxed on that extra $2 million at a rate of 45% upon her death. That's a $900,000 tax bill to Kitty's heirs, whether they are Adam, Hoss, Little Joe, Hop Sing, or Jesse and Frank James.

On the other hand, Ben's $2 million in the Bypass Trust is not only tax exempt from Kitty's estate, but even if it appreciates in value over the years, all of the appreciation will not be taxed as income to the three sons. **There is no estate tax on the increased value of the Bypass Trust.**

Kitty can be the trustee of the Bypass Trust and may even be able to invade the corpus of the trust if she can show a "reasonable need" for her "health, support, education, and maintenance." However, if any of the appreciated assets are sold while she is alive, she, or the three sons, will still have to pay a capital gains tax on the appreciated income.

This is where you can see trouble brewing. Whether or not a trip to Europe would be a reasonable need for Kitty, is the big question. The Bypass Trust becomes irrevocable upon the death of Ben, and Kitty has no power to change the beneficiaries named in the trust document. Therefore, Adam, Hoss, or Little Joe could bring a lawsuit against Kitty to stop her from invading the trust corpus and wasting the assets to pay for her traveling expenses.

Not allowing Kitty to change the beneficiaries in the Bypass Trust, keeps the money from going into the hands of the wrong people, at least, in the mind of the deceased Ben. But he can not dictate from the grave. Ben has no control over how much of the trust will actually be left when Kitty dies. He has no control over Kitty's spending. But a separate trustee, other than Kitty or the boys, would have control over the spending, and that might be a good idea.

Some spouses are justifiably concerned about their spouse's spending habits. In those instances, a QTIP Trust may be an appropriate alternative to the Bypass Trust, or a thoughtful addition to the estate plan, to make certain the previous adult children get their inheritance.

QTIP Trust
(Qualified Terminable Interest Property)

The QTIP Trust can be as complicated as the acronym implies but is widely used as an estate planning tool. There are specific requirements that must be met based on the Internal Revenue Code. For example, all of the income from the trust must go to the surviving spouse for life and there can be no one with authority to alter that.

A QTIP is valuable because it is the only form of "marital deduction" that gives the husband control over the disposition of the trust property after his wife dies, by distributing it to his specified beneficiaries. The property interest is called "terminable" because it ends upon the wife's death.

As a "marital deduction" any amount of money can be added to the QTIP Trust from husband's estate, tax-free. But upon his wife's death the remainder of the QTIP Trust is added back into her estate and will be taxed if it is over her $2 million tax exemption.

Thus, in Kitty's case the $500,000 remainder in the QTIP Trust will be added back into her gross estate when she dies and be taxed at 45% on all amounts over the "applicable exclusion amount" which we know is $2 million in 2008. (This language is technical but it is the language that will be used in the estate documents.)

For example, if Ben Cartwright's share of the Bonanza estate was $2 million in community property and $500,000 in separate property, he may want to put the $2 million into the Bypass Trust. This trust would provide money for Kitty's "health, support, education and maintenance." It would also save Kitty's heirs $900,000 in estate taxes upon her death in 2008, because the $2 million in the Bypass Trust would "bypass" Kitty's estate and go directly to the named heirs in that trust. These beneficiaries would receive the remainder of the money in the trust tax free. As for the $500,000 in the QTIP Trust, after the taxes were paid on it by Kitty's named heirs with the money from her own trust, if necessary, it would then pass directly to Ben's three sons, tax free.

Kitty will receive an annual income from the QTIP Trust generated from the $500,000, but she is not allowed to invade the core assets of the trust for any reason. These core assets are also referred to as the corpus, assets, principal, funds, property, money, remainder, etc. Upon her death, the "remainder" of the trust, as explained above, avoids probate and goes directly to the beneficiaries. It is also free from Kitty's creditors, and automatically passes to Adam, Hoss, and Little Joe with no further fanfare. The fact that the remainder is free from creditors is an important point if Kitty turns out to be a big spender.

Kitty's heirs to her Survivor's Trust pick up the tax bill on the amount over $2 million that may be added back into her estate from the QTIP. The bottom line is that the QTIP Trust only defers taxes on the $500,000 from Ben's estate. But if Kitty's Survivor's Trust has dwindled in value down to $1.5 million before the QTIP is added back into it after her death, there would be no taxes to pay on her estate.

By using the QTIP Trust, Ben has assured himself that his sons will receive at least $500,000, of his estate regardless of how Kitty's spending habits might otherwise affect it.

Ben's primary concern may secretly have been that because Kitty is still a young and attractive woman, she may remarry and not feel compelled to leave as much of the Bonanza to Adam, Hoss, and Little Joe as Ben would have liked. The QTIP becomes irrevocable upon Ben's death and cannot be changed.

Special Needs Trust

A Special Needs Trust (SNT) is designed to allow a person living with a disability to receive money into a trust from several sources and still maintain their eligibility for government assistance.

There was no need for a SNT in the Cartwright family.

Most government aid programs require the recipient to have resources and income below a certain level, such as Social Security insurance, Medicaid, IHSS, subsidy housing (Section 8), and state, federal and local benefits. In other words, the federal programs provide aid to special needs people with no financial resources larger than $2,000. However, that does not mean you cannot set up a SNT for someone who is less fortunate.

For example, when a disabled person receives an inheritance gift or a substantial personal injury award, they have three choices. They can: 1) go off assistance, 2) spend it all until they are poor again, or 3) get a SNT.

The SNT allows the trustee to fund money for the purchase of certain items which are not deemed by the government as "financial resources." This would include a home of any value, a vehicle of any value, household goods, and other social and medical services available to the disabled person.

Preparing the Special Needs Trust requires the attorney to be familiar with the government program's specific requirements the beneficiary may be eligible for, and that can be difficult in the midst of constantly changing law. It is not something you want to take a chance on yourself and because your loved one could become ineligible for aid.

Nevertheless, the SNT can be the perfect tool in the right situation and should be considered if you have money and a disabled parent, child or friend.

What To Do With This Information

With the information you have just read, go forward and study the two Revocable Trusts to reevaluate the decisions made by Ben and Kitty Cartwright as exhibited on their own flow chart. Think about how the definitions of the trusts we have just learned would work for them. How would it work for you? Do you have a prenuptial agreement or have you entered into a transmutation agreement? Look at all the boxes and follow the arrows to their destination, and/or their alternative destination until you understand how it works.

If you take the time to do so, it becomes clear how the tools of estate planning can work for you. This is a prototype for every estate plan, including very large estates or very moderate estates. More sophisticated tools will be presented when learning how to plan for the larger estates, whether this means family members or assets.

To help visually enhance your understanding of this process, following are two "BONANZA" flow charts. The first one applies to Kitty and the boys if she continues to live out the "traditional" lifestyle and finds a man who either she loves, or who might be taking advantage of her. The second chart applies to a lifestyle where she remarries and goes her separate way.

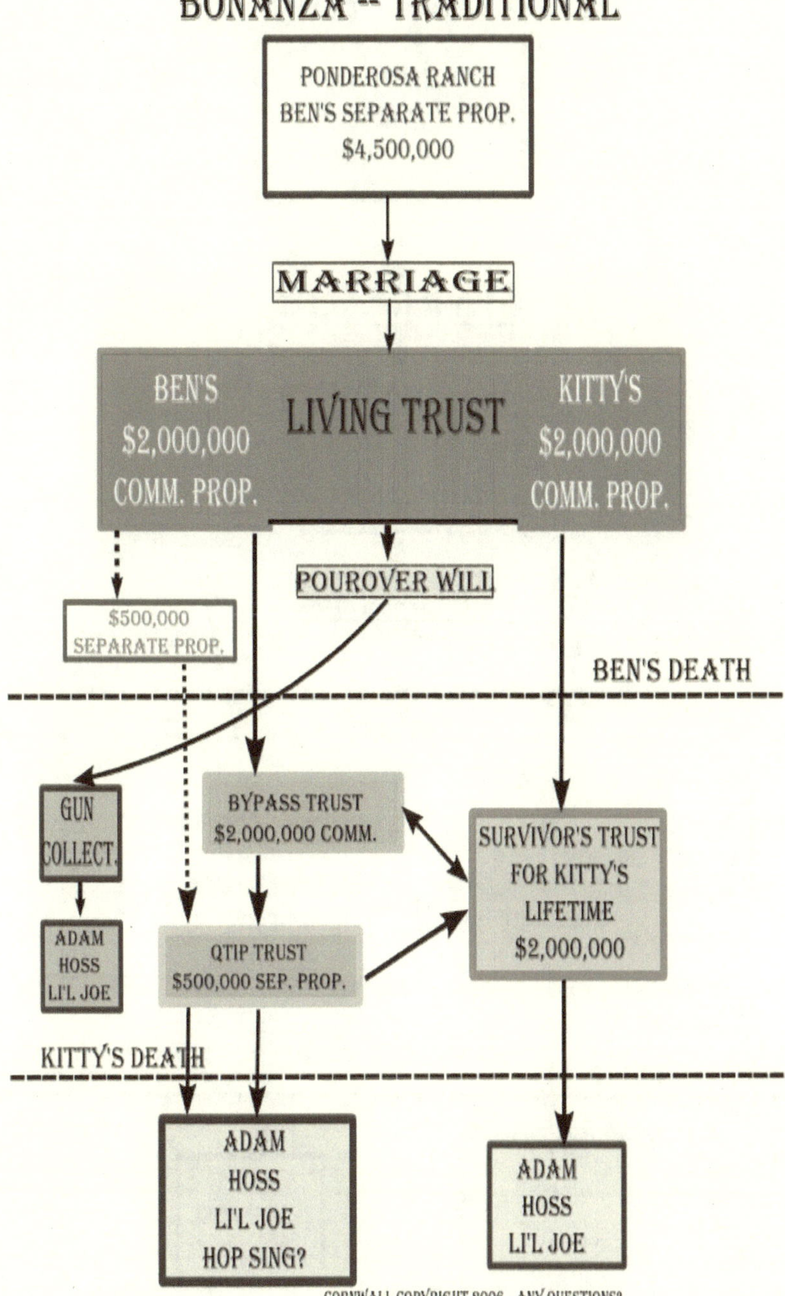
BONANZA -- TRADITIONAL
PONDEROSA RANCH
BEN'S SEPARATE PROP.
$4,500,000
MARRIAGE
BEN'S
$2,000,000
COMM. PROP.
LIVING TRUST
KITTY'S
$2,000,000
COMM. PROP.
POUROVER WILL
$500,000
SEPARATE PROP.
BEN'S DEATH
GUN
COLLECT.
BYPASS TRUST
$2,000,000 COMM.
SURVIVOR'S TRUST
FOR KITTY'S
LIFETIME
$2,000,000
ADAM
HOSS
LI'L JOE
QTIP TRUST
$500,000 SEP. PROP.
KITTY'S DEATH
ADAM
HOSS
LI'L JOE
HOP SING?
ADAM
HOSS
LI'L JOE
CORNWALL COPYRIGHT 2006 --ANY QUESTIONS?

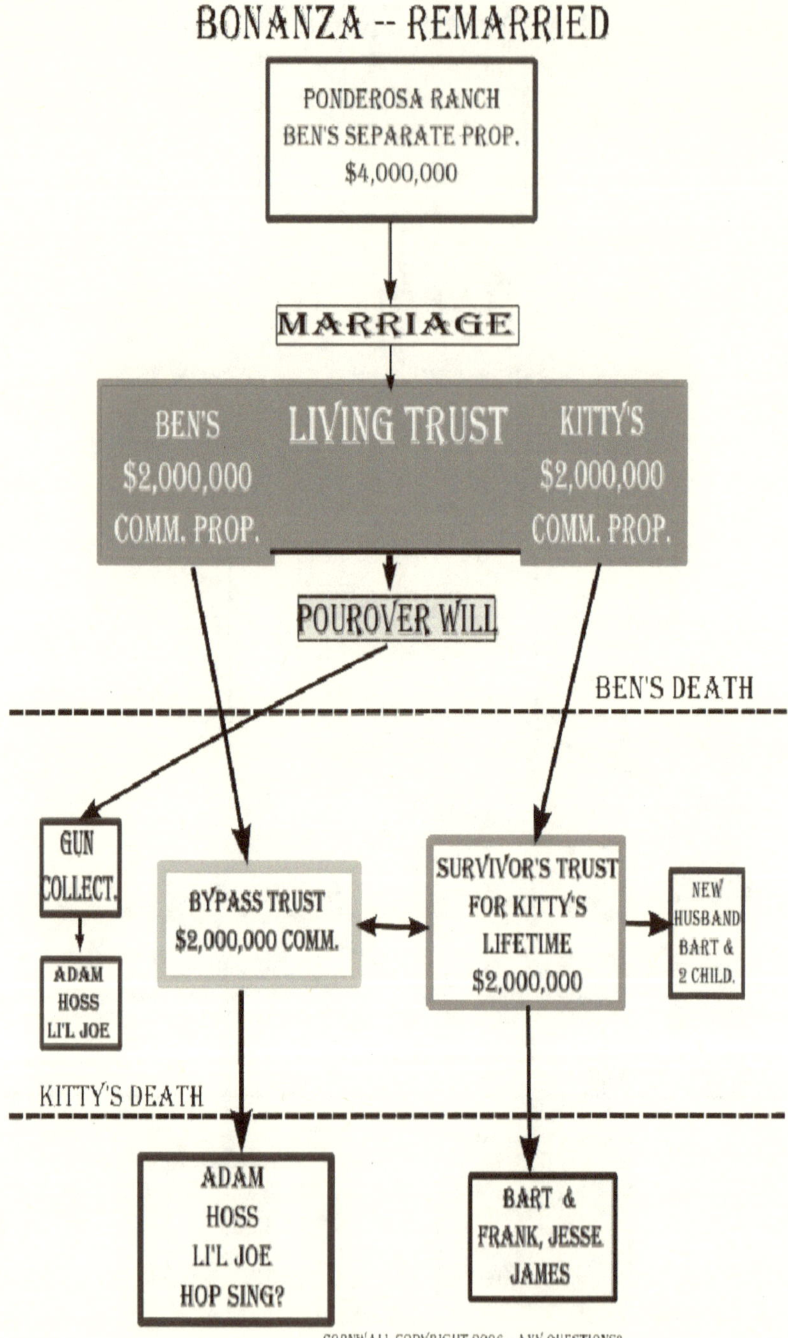
BONANZA -- REMARRIED
PONDEROSA RANCH
BEN'S SEPARATE PROP.
$4,000,000
MARRIAGE
BEN'S
$2,000,000
COMM. PROP.
LIVING TRUST
KITTY'S
$2,000,000
COMM. PROP.
POUROVER WILL
BEN'S DEATH
GUN
COLLECT.
ADAM
HOSS
LI'L JOE
BYPASS TRUST
$2,000,000 COMM.
SURVIVOR'S TRUST
FOR KITTY'S
LIFETIME
$2,000,000
NEW
HUSBAND
BART &
2 CHILD.
KITTY'S DEATH
ADAM
HOSS
LI'L JOE
HOP SING?
BART &
FRANK, JESSE
JAMES
CORNWALL COPYRIGHT 2006 --ANY QUESTIONS?

CHAPTER TWELVE

Dealing With Your Family Dynamic

It is estimated 60% or more of the population lives in a blended family. The term "blended family" is a modern term of art we use in the legal field. It includes that family where the parents are on their second or third marriage, have their children, their step-children, and perhaps children together.

The step children may live in the same house, or there could be adult children who live out of the home. There could be a large disparity in age with the new children. They have little in common with these younger children because ten or twenty years might have passed since the first or second marriage ended, which means there is a wife # 1, and/or a husband #2, etc. Think what would happen if Mike and Carol of the Brady Bunch divorced and remarried a third partner.

In the dictionary, the word "blended" is defined as "to mix smoothly and inseparably together." Given that definition, and the character of the typical "blended family," the term should probably be changed to "unblended family."

Dynamics like the age differences between children of prior marriages and the new children may breed animosity. Petty jealousies can arise. There was less money in the estate when the older children were young, and perhaps the new spouse brought wealth to the marriage that the older children mistakenly believe they have a right to.

Now they are young adults and their own wealth status and desires are dissimilar to the needs of the new minor children. And of course, the adult children's loyalty is to their own mother.

From a litigator's point of view, this family is living in a volatile world and is subject to "probable litigation" upon the death of the first spouse. This can happen whether the estate has something to fight over, or not. The best way to understand what to do in the blended family situation is to understand what will happen if you do nothing. Remember that all of us have an estate plan whether we like it or not.

The State of California, as with every state, has devised a plan that will distribute your assets upon your death in accordance with the rules of intestate succession found in the Probate Code.

All you have to do for these rules to apply to you is to die without a Will or some other non-probate estate plan. This is called to die "intestate." This means the beneficiaries of your estate will be identified by statute and fixed by the court, rather than by you.

The legislative policy for "intestate succession" (to whom your property goes) reflects a paternal instinct in the law to protect and provide for the surviving spouse and minor children. This policy is designed for the "traditional family."

There are even laws to protect the welfare of the decedent's surviving family, to the exclusion of named beneficiaries in a Will, or against creditors, if it appears they will exhaust the estate of individuals in the family who are protected by law, i.e. the surviving wife and children.

This is all fine and good for the traditional family of hard working Bruce, and stay at home mom Kathy Jones. They have been happily married for twenty-five years, and have two healthy boys whom they love dearly. If Bruce dies, the estate will go to Kathy, and after she dies, to the two children equally -- no problem.

But what about the older Tom and younger Cindy Smith? Tom is 60 years old and Cindy is 40. Tom has two adult sons from a previous marriage of twenty-five years, and two grandchildren. Cindy and Tom have been married five years and have a three year old daughter.

If Tom dies without a Will or Trust, his adult children will be surprised to find that Cindy is in control of everything, and is entitled to most of their father's estate. This is regardless of how much separate property their father took into the marriage with him.

The new wife will end up with all the community property and as much as two-thirds of Tom's separate property. This happens as follows:

According to the laws of intestate succession in California, as followed in most states, Cindy is entitled to all of the community property; including Tom's half of the community. That part you may have suspected. But as Tom's wife at the time of his death, she is also entitled to one-third of his separate property, regardless of where it came from or how large its value.

In addition, Tom's three year old daughter is also entitled to one-third of the remaining two-thirds of Tom's separate property, which she will share equally with his two sons. But because the daughter is a minor, her share will pass directly to Cindy. **Therefore, Cindy is entitled to all of the community property and almost two-thirds of Tom's separate property regardless of the amount of value.**

As you can see, these default laws greatly benefit the surviving spouse and/or children of the "traditional family." In the case of Tom and Cindy the laws give no consideration to Tom's grandchildren, and little thought to the sons from his previous marriage.

What's more, as Tom's executor Cindy is entitled to take an administrative fee, which is equal to the fee of the attorney she hires, and she also inherits the "power of appointment" over the estate. That means she determines who the heirs of Tom's separate property will be, as long as she leaves a Will or Revocable Trust.

In other words, Cindy is not holding Tom's property in a life estate which would pass to his children or grandchildren when she dies. It is all Cindy's, and in all fairness it cannot be thought of as Tom's anymore since he gave it away, albeit unintentionally.

Unfortunately, this can be a difficult pill for Tom's older children to swallow. Had his wishes been otherwise, Tom could have drawn up a simple estate plan that distributed his life's earnings more evenly. In my father's case, all he received from his father's new wife as his entire inheritance was an old tea pot warmer. I still have it as a reminder.

Leaving It to the Children

As for leaving money to children, there is much to take into consideration depending on the age and temperament of the child. The older you get, the more outrageous it seems to leave a large sum of money to an eighteen year old.

It is commonly recommended that a trust be used to stagger payments, possibly at the ages of 23, 26, and 30. The expectation is that at 23 your son will want to buy a Porsche, at 26 he will have graduated college, and at 30 he will have settled down and knows what he wants to do in life. For others, the ages of 20, 30 and 40 sound more appropriate.

Yet some parents may want to provide for their children's education and then leave the rest of the money to charity. This is easily accomplished through a wonderful tax saving device known as a "charitable remainder unitrust" (CRUT).

A CRUT is very flexible and will allow you to, among other things; sell stocks with a very low tax basis at a very, very high price, and not pay any capital gains taxes on the appreciation of the stock. It works the same for highly appreciated real estate. As you will see, whether used to pay for the education of your children, or to provide a percentage of the income to you for retirement, a CRUT is a valuable tool in estate planning. (See Chapter Sixteen for more details on CRUTs).

The normal prerequisite of a trust for children is that it protects the *corpus* (that amount of money in the trust) from them; thus the name "Spendthrift Trusts."

Another way of helping a young adult manage their money, rather than keeping it from them, or forcing it on them, is to allow them to withdraw money from the trust as they believe they need it. This essentially allows them to be their own trustee without the responsibility of managing the entire sum of money in the trust.

Another way to manage children's money is to establish a Family Pot Trust that can be distributed to each child in accordance to their needs, according to the trustee's discretion or by the terms in the trust. Another way is a Minor's Trust; another is a Custodial Account, and there are more.

Therefore, as you can envision, there are many ways to plan your child's inheritance. Most parents are afraid a trust may be a distraction for a young person. They believe it might rob the children of their incentive to go out in the world and do well. More than one child has been lured away from college, or taken up a life of drugs, because the easy money was there with no conditions required before they get the money.

These concerns can be relieved by language in the trust that stops money when the child is not enrolled in college full time, fails to maintain a certain grade point average, gets arrested more than once, or violates some other standard of conduct that was outlined in the trust.

Transferring Your Parent's House To You Creates A Capital Gains Conundrum

In the majority of cases where the parent transfers a house to their child during their lifetime, it creates a capital gains conundrum. The child receives an immediate benefit when receiving the house because the state does not reassess the value of the home for tax purposes on a parent-child transfer. (It doesn't reassess on a child-parent transfer either.) Therefore, the child pays no increased property tax. But, if the child wants to sell the house their parents gifted to them, they are going to be hard hit by long term capital gains.

Suppose your parents bought a three bedroom house in 1956 for $10,000 and it is now worth $880,000. Those are very realistic numbers in southern California. Your parents have been renting the house for profit during the last three years, and now decide to gift the house to you.

When they transfer the title to you, there will be no change in the cost basis of the house. Your parents cost basis carries over to you and therefore you pay no higher property tax on the property than they did. Your cost basis is $10,000.

What happens if you want to sell the property? With a cost basis of $10,000, you would pay capital gains tax on an $870,000 gain after a sale for $880,000.

The federal capital gains tax brackets are complex and shifting, but as of this writing in 2008, the gain on property sold on or after May 6, 2003, is taxed at a rate over 15%.

The California state income tax brackets are the same as the state capital gains brackets. Therefore, a single person with a capital gain of over $40,000, and a married couple with a capital gain of over $80,000 will pay the highest rate of tax California has which is 9.3%.

The math on the property works out as follows:

$880,000 fair market value
$880,000 sale
- $10,000 cost basis
$870,000 gain
- 15% Fed. tax = $130,500
- 9.3% state tax = $80,910

You will be responsible for paying $211,410 in taxes if you sold the house at today's fair market price. It takes many years of property tax to add up to that number.

One alternative to paying these taxes is to wait to inherit the property after your parent's death. At that point there will be a "step up" of the cost basis to the fair market value of the house today. The cost basis of $10,000 will step up to the sale price of $880,000.

If you sell your parents' house immediately after their death, there would be no capital gains taxes on the sale, if the house did not appreciate in value from the date of death.

This would all seem a little callous if you actually put gift deferment and tax avoidance ahead of the death of your parents. But the beauty of estate planning is recognizing the financial reality of these basic tax consequences and making the best of them -- and not being rudely surprised.

For example, according to IRC 121, if a married couple has owned *and* occupied a house for two out of the last five years, they can exclude the first $500,000 of their capital gain from taxes. (It is $250,000 for a single person.)

In the scenario above, your parents could have sold the house they moved from three years ago and paid taxes on only $370,000, reducing the tax bill to $89,910, and saving $121,500 for you.

And if a single homeowner was required to move into a nursing facility due to health reasons they can deduct the first $250,000 of capital gain if they lived in the house one out of the previous five years.

CHAPTER THIRTEEN

Planning the Larger Estate

It is a common misconception that estate planning is only for the wealthy. In the preceding twelve chapters, I have explained why every Baby Boomer needs to plan their estate. The misconception that you have to be wealthy to put the time and money into planning the distribution of your estate should be dispelled. Afterall, since you spent fifty years working, it's worth more than a couple of hours thought, and a few hundred bucks, to organize your estate and go out in style. "Hero" style.

Of course estate planning is essential for those who have accumulated substantial wealth, but it is also imperative for those of modest or moderate wealth as well. Every dollar lost unnecessarily, to taxes or administrative costs, hurts the survivors more when the estate is small and the government takes 55% of it.

The Titanic of Estate Planning: Rupert Murdoch

The Titanic of all estate planning would fall on the shoulders of a man as big as Rupert Murdoch, the world's 109th wealthiest man in 2008. But he is number one when it comes to his bewildering family dynamic and his failure to devise an acceptable plan for distributing his billions of dollars amongst his heirs.

Mr. Murdoch is the 77 year old media mogul with a "net" estate value of $8.3 billion according to *Forbes.* He owns such companies as the *Fox Network*, the *New York Post*, along with the recent addition of the *Wall Street Journal* and its parent company Dow Jones. This all comprises his multi-national company, which includes a mind boggling 188 other publications under the company name, the "News Corporation."

He has billions of dollars in assets throughout the world - particularly in Australia, (he is Australian born, but is a U.S. citizen) New Zealand, Britain and America. He is a former owner of the LA Dodgers baseball team, which never quite worked for him like the purchase of MySpace.com.

Mr. Murdoch's blended family includes four adult children, and two infant children. These six children are his daughter Prudence by his first marriage; Elizabeth, Lachlan and James by his second marriage which ended in 1999; and Grace 3, and Chloe 2, from his current marriage in 2005.

Mr. Murdoch has recently announced that all his children will be treated equally in the distribution of his estate, and he gave the sum of $600 million to his six children last year for estate planning purposes. It is difficult to know the motivation behind the advanced distribution of $600 million. Let's hope it made them happy. Particularly since rumor has it the heir apparent, his eldest son Lachlan, age 35, who quit the family business in 2005, may or may not be coming back on board. His reason for leaving was the sweeping changes his father made in his estate plan in 2006.

The 2006 plan allegedly makes the third wife, Wendi Deng, the most powerful player in the family trust because she will act as guardian for her two infant daughters until they can claim their inheritance at age 30. That's three votes for Wendi, and only one vote for each of the adult children.

This new property distribution plan also invalidates the previous deal Murdoch struck with his second wife, Anna, during their divorce proceedings in 1999. That deal granted Anna's children, along with Prudence from the first marriage, control of the trust in the event of Murdoch's death. The new deal substantially reduces the power of Mr. Murdoch's four adult children to...well, less than they want.

More recently in March of 2008, Mr. Murdoch was apparently guilt ridden for having his 99 year-old mother buy shares in *News Corporation* so he could inherit them through the company. He recently determined the dividends of *News Corporation* under his control, are so paltry that he had short changed his mother $273 million dollars between the years 1984 to 1994. She apparently could have made $273 million more if she had invested in higher yielding stocks.

Therefore, he agreed to pay his mother back $85 million out of guilt, improper advice, or lack of care, but the problem is that it ignited a taxable event causing the 99 year-old mother to pay $70 million dollars in taxes. This issue was before the court in March, and where the tax collectors were attempting to collect in New York City.

Things must be tough up there in the big leagues and it would be nice to think that $8.3 "net" billion in trust for all the beneficiaries to share could make them happy. But who knows? If the dynamics of this blended family spiral out of control and into the "exploding turkey scenario" (where the family goes crazy over the holiday season) there will be enough legal work here to keep a thousand attorneys fighting into the next millennium. And you thought your situation was diverse, volatile, or downright complicated!

Big Concepts for Big Challenges

People in Mr. Murdoch's league have buildings full of attorneys. However, estate planning is not like business law because it requires substantially different skills. It requires attorneys who have affirmative people skills, not adversarial skills, and the ability to listen and work personally with the client.

It is not the intent of this book to provide sufficient legal knowledge for you to write your own estate plan. You would have to go to law school, and then practice trust law for twenty years in order to do that right. It can get quite complicated and demand the use of several professionals working in coordination. The information provided here is only intended to stimulate ideas so you can better understand your needs and communicate them to your attorney.

As your estate grows larger, and the marital tax exemption grows smaller, the more need there is for using the various tools allowed by the Internal Revenue Code in order to sculpt your estate into a work of legal art. However, every estate is different. Consider the different family needs that must be served between Dr. Dentist and Walt the Plumbing Contractor (pseudonyms for real people), as they plan their estate.

CHAPTER FOURTEEN

Two Successful Baby Boomers' Visions

A. Dr. Dentist is 58 years old and still married to his first wife, Nora. They have two minor daughters in private school and live in a 10,000 square foot home on an exclusive golf course. They buy a new car any time they want. Both the girls are equestrian riders and Nora is busy managing their home, the kids and charity events.

The doctor has a twin engine Golden Eagle airplane he uses to commute to his other lucrative dental practice in another town. Besides their residence, they own a cabin in Lake Tahoe and a large medical office in downtown Santa Barbara. He has five other dentist working for him. Dr. Dentist has received good financial advice over the years and developed a well rounded securities portfolio worth over $2 million.

Besides his own IRA and 401k for the office, he has set aside money for his daughter's educational fund. Dr. Dentist also provides for his mother who lives nearby and who is in her eighties.

Here is one way to do their plan:

DR. DENTIST AND NORA

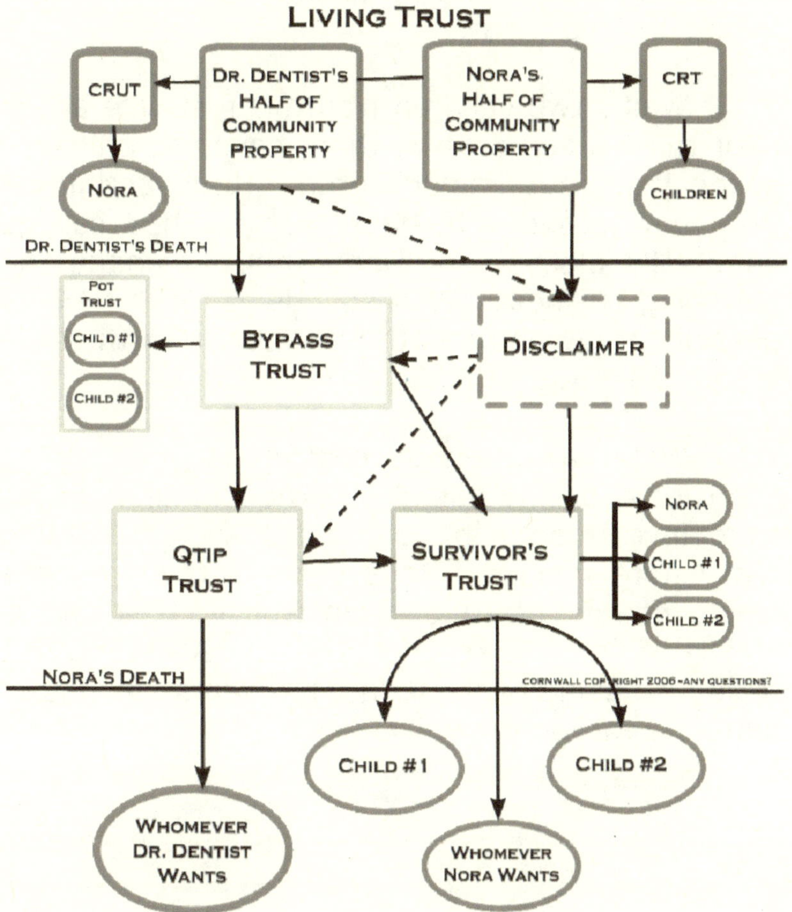

B. Walt the Plumbing Contractor is 58 years old and has been working in the plumbing business for thirty-five years. He recently married his third wife. He has two former wives with whom he shares four adult children, but he has always been the only parent with the financial means to help them.

Walt's two children from his first wife are in their thirties and each of them have two children, giving Walt four grandchildren. His two children from his second wife have just reached college age. His oldest son, Derek helps manage the plumbing business. Walt spends as much time as possible at his home in the Caribbean on the little island of *Paraiso*.

Walt has been successful as a plumbing contractor, but he has also earned windfall profits from investments in California's ever increasing real estate market. Regardless of the presently falling market of 2008, from which it will take a couple of years to recover, the appreciation in his residence alone over the last ten years has netted him $1.2 million in equity.

There is also a condo up the coast he purchased in 1990 for $125,000, that is now worth $425,000. He owns an old office building in the Five Cities that he bought in 1992 for $475,000, and after redevelopment of its commercial space, is now worth $2.2 million dollars. Those, along with a couple rental houses he owns and rents, makes his "net" value in real estate $3.5 million.

The appraised value used by the probate court is the "gross" value of his properties, which, if he died today, would be $5.5 million. On top of that is the appraised value of the plumbing business and equipment.

If you wondered which of these scenarios is most challenging, the answer would be they are equally the same. They are juxtaposed with the same level of individual complexity, but they have little in common with the other after that.

Dr. Dentist and Walt's primary needs go in opposite directions. Dr. Dentist's primary need is to provide for his wife and the future of his minor children (referred to above as the "traditional family").

Walt has recently remarried, after toiling 35 years to build his estate. His "primary" need may be is to provide for his adult children and grandchildren, while assuring security for his new wife. Walt's situation is something of a balancing act.

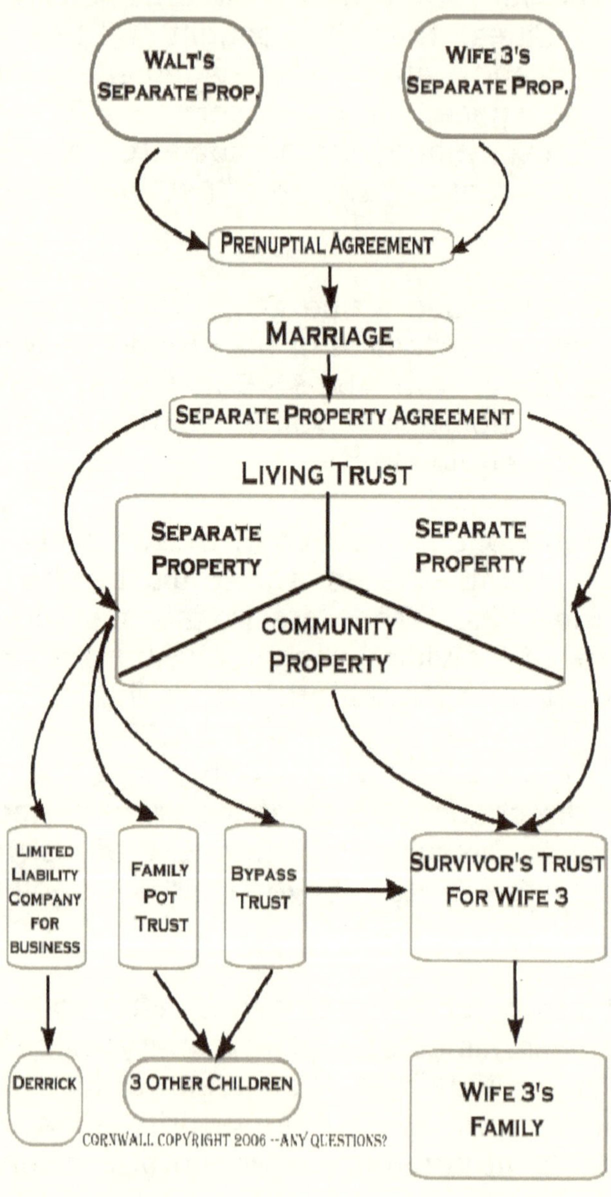
WALT THE PLUMBING CONTRACTOR
WALT'S SEPARATE PROP.
WIFE 3'S SEPARATE PROP.
PRENUPTIAL AGREEMENT
MARRIAGE
SEPARATE PROPERTY AGREEMENT
LIVING TRUST
SEPARATE PROPERTY
SEPARATE PROPERTY
COMMUNITY PROPERTY
LIMITED LIABILITY COMPANY FOR BUSINESS
FAMILY POT TRUST
BYPASS TRUST
SURVIVOR'S TRUST FOR WIFE 3
DERRICK
3 OTHER CHILDREN
WIFE 3'S FAMILY
CORNWALL COPYRIGHT 2006 --ANY QUESTIONS?

In addition to the trust tools discussed in Chapter Ten, the larger estates may want to utilize more specialized tools, such as a "three-way formula split with a marital deduction pecuniary formula clause," and a "Disclaimer Trust" as well as a "reverse QTIP Trust," and definitely a "Sprinkling Trust," (also called a "Family Pot Trust") for the children, with distribution in three stages. A trust in two stages for his children from his two previous marriages, and/or a Generation Skipping Trust might be helpful. And, of course, a Charitable Remainder Trust. Okay, got that, because there is more?

On the business side of things it may be necessary to have a Buy-Out Agreement with business partners, or perhaps business would be best served by transferring ownership into a LLC or a corporation, and your family property or business property go into a FLC; and on, and on it can go.

These more sophisticated wealth transfer tools are discussed below, but, at this level, you only need to know how it works and what it is called. The actual writing of these two Revocable Trusts have become very complicated in recent years because the documents are intended to be scrutinized by the court or the IRS. Just make certain your attorney has malpractice insurance in case they make a big mistake. They are not supposed to make mistakes, but how would you know unless you understood what the 35-page document was putting into action to preserve your legacy? The more formidable problem is if the first to die did most of the planning, and still doesn't know what a QTIP Trust is or how it affects the estate of the surviving spouse. In that case, the surviving spouse is the one left to figure out if an error has been made or not. The surviving spouse may not like the way the QTIP doubles her estate value which forces her heirs to pay the additional estate tax.

That is why the more you learn the better the entire family will benefit.

CHAPTER FIFTEEN

Sophisticated Legal Terms

This book does not use any legal terms in helping the reader understand Revocable Trust that are not the most up to date terminology used in the business. Confusion can arise when attorneys use different terms to describe the same estate planning tool. This is due in large part to attorneys using the terms they learned in law school thirty years ago. The use of the terms "A Trust" and "B Trust" is one example. Those terms were popular until too many cases came back to be probated because the attorneys were getting them mixed up.

Many terms used in this book might sound like some archaic lexicon from ages past, but to a certain extent that is exactly what legal language is. It was never intended to be used in the vernacular, and it is nearly impossible to translate some of them without losing meaning in the translation and confusing the layperson.

Nevertheless, the idea in this book is to breed familiarity with the language that will be used in the legal documents which will divide and distribute your estate after you or your spouse is gone. Hopefully that will help you understand the Revocable Trust or Will before you sign anything. If you did not want to know more about the legal "terms of art," such as Bypass Trust, or Survivor's Trust, you would not be reading this book.

At the risk of being criticized for oversimplifying the definitions of complex legal concepts, or perhaps applauded for doing the same, there are some terms you need to know to better understand how estate planning works. Only three days ago I was giving a speech at a Women's Association, and I asked, "Can you imagine going into an attorney's office and paying him to explain what a QTIP Trust is?" I doubt he could do it easily because attorneys are used to having their legal terms of art go unquestioned, and they have never really thought about the easiest way to explain what a QTIP Trust is, along with its ramifications. It has been my experience that when a client is paying by the hour for legal services, they prefer to take the word of the attorney rather then pay for an explanation of it. This, unfortunately, is what drives many an estate plan.

At the end of my speech a woman said she would buy the book because she had a QTIP Trust in her estate plan and had no idea what it meant.

Here are some brief descriptions of the terms mentioned above in the estates of Dr. Dentist and Walt the Plumber. To make it simpler assume that in every case the husband has died first. "Husband" is much easier than the term of art, "deceased settlor."

"The Three-Way Formula Split With Marital Deduction Pecuniary Formula Clause"

You may think you will never run across a phrase like this in your estate plan, but in fact the clause is used frequently in Revocable Trusts. Its purpose is to determine how much of the deceased husband's estate goes directly to the wife, and how much of the estate assets will fund the Bypass Trust.

Generically speaking, a "marital deduction formula clause" splits the husband's and wife's estate into two parts: the marital deduction share goes to the wife's Survivor's Trust, and the nonmarital exemption share goes into the deceased husband's "Credit Shelter Trust" e.g. Bypass Trust, to be used by wife for her lifetime, then distributed to the children upon her death.

Remember that the wife is entitled by law to receive all of her husband's estate directly into her Survivor's Trust if he dies intestate. She will not pay a penny of taxes, even if it was a billion dollars. This is called the "unlimited marital deduction."

This "unlimited marital deduction" as opposed to a "marital deduction formula clause" could produce horrendous results. It would be a very expensive mistake for a wealthy wife to accept all of her husband's estate into her own estate because their children would pay a whopper of a tax on it when she dies, assuming it is over $1 million in 2011.

The marital deduction formula clause divides the husband's property between the wife's Survivor's Trust and his Bypass Trust by using a formula. The most popular formula for dividing up the property interest is called a "pecuniary marital formula."

It is the most popular because it avoids many of the pitfalls created when dividing property by a fractional interest formula, or by direct gifting.

For example, if you split up the husband's estate fractionally, with one-half of an asset going to the Survivor's Trust and one-half going to the Bypass Trust, you could end up with co-ownership of the asset between hostile family members.

Pecuniary means "money" and when the husband's estate is divided by a pecuniary formula it means that upon his death a certain amount of his monetary interest "under the formula" is going to be allocated to the Survivor's Trust, or the Bypass Trust, or even the QTIP Trust.

Unlike the fractional formula clause, the pecuniary formula clause allows the trustee (the surviving spouse normally) to "pick and choose" the assets that will go into the specific trust. This means the asset must be evaluated before it can be distributed to the trust, then it is put in one trust or the other as a whole asset, not as a fractioned asset.

The amount of pecuniary interest that will be allocated to the Survivor's Trust, or the Bypass Trust, will read something like this: "The trustee shall distribute to the Bypass Trust the smallest pecuniary amount so as to result in the least tax paid, and produce the optimum marital deduction for the estate of the surviving spouse." The goal is to achieve the most favorable tax treatment.

This allows the trustee, Nora in the case of Dr. Dentist, to select specific assets from the estate to fund the marital and nonmarital shares of the estate. She gets maximum flexibility of "picking and choosing" specific assets in order to get the best tax results. Not only does she allocate specific property to go into specific trusts, but she chooses which assets to keep for her own trust.

The major benefit, is that she can efficiently tailor her share of the estate to receive the most favorable income tax results during her lifetime, and then for her children after she is gone. She can also decide exactly which asset may best satisfy an individual beneficiary's needs (such as her two daughters) and put those assets into the Bypass Trust. These may be highly appreciating stocks that would only increase the size of Nora's estate, which she does not need, but that would be great for her children's future.

Because Nora does not have to make the marital deduction election until after Dr. Dentist dies, she will have a clearer picture of the financial reality than what might have existed when she and the doctor had the Will or Trust drafted, perhaps years before his death.

A "three way formula split" is applicable where there is a Revocable Trust created by two married persons, such as Dr. Dentist and Nora. Typically, when they establish their Revocable Trust, it will contain both their community property as well as their separate property. When Dr. Dentist dies it may be necessary to divide the Revocable Trust property into three shares.

When a three-way division is made, there will be a "marital deduction share," a "nonmarital share," and a "survivor's share" which consists of Nora's separate property plus her share of their community property. This three-way split preserves the distinction between Nora's property and the property that formerly belonged to Dr. Dentist. This facilitates different treatment of those two categories of property, which is beyond the scope of this discussion.

It is important to note, this three-way split may be more helpful to an estate like Walt the Plumber. Since Walt recently remarried, there has been no time to accumulate community property. We know he comes into the relationship with a substantial amount of separate property. If his new wife also came into the marriage with substantial separate property to leave to her family, then a three-way split may be the best way to organize their estate.

However, the "marital deduction pecuniary formula clause" has no place in the distribution of Walt's estate. It would not be advisable to leave the "picking and choosing" of the assets selected for the benefit of his children to the discretion of his new wife. Under normal conditions, that is not the wise thing to do. It is recommended a different trustee be used for the job.

It would be best if Walt and his new wife entered into an "Agreement Between Spouses Regarding Status of Property." In this way, the entire issue could be spelled out for the survivor.

Disclaimer Trust

A marital deduction pecuniary clause, or "formula clause" and a Disclaimer Trust operate in much the same way. They both give Nora the advantage of "picking and choosing" assets she may or may not want in her own estate now that she is single.

The difference is a "formula clause" controls how much of her husband's estate shall be distributed into each Bypass or QTIP Trust, while a Disclaimer Trust allows her to keep her husband's entire estate if she chooses.

Along with this power to choose comes the "power of appointment" allowing her to bequeath and devise her husband's share of the estate the way she wants. This power over her husband's assets also makes her vulnerable to the interpretation that the assets should be included back into her estate for tax purposes.

In our example where Dr. Dentist dies first, a Disclaimer Trust is used to help the surviving Nora tailor her own estate to gain the most favorable income tax advantage. The Disclaimer Trust operates the same as a Credit Shelter Trust (Bypass Trust) only it is funded differently.

Instead of the trust being irrevocably funded upon the death of Dr. Dentist by way of a marital deduction formula, Nora has the opportunity to decide how much of Dr. Dentist's share of the estate she wants to accept into her own estate, or how much of the property she does not accept (disclaims) because of the poor tax result to her surviving estate.

Nora would then pass the disclaimed property on to the doctor's Credit Shelter Trust (now called a "Disclaimer Trust") and she could become a lifetime beneficiary of the trust income, as well as have a right to invade the principal of the trust.

The allure of the Disclaimer Trust is that it allows Nora to postpone the issue of the size of the "Credit Shelter Trust" she will fund from her husband's estate, until after he dies. At the time they sign their Will or Revocable Trust, there may be some uncertainty about how large Dr. Dentist's separate estate may actually be years later when he dies. Currently, we also have uncertainty about the estate tax, and a Disclaimer Trust can provide that needed flexibility.

If his estate has downturns and is sufficiently small, Nora may want it all to pass into her estate because there will be no significant tax result. But if it has substantially grown over the years, she may want to disclaim a portion and put it in the Credit Shelter Trust to preserve for her, and perhaps "sprinkle" for the benefit of her children. Given the size of Dr. Dentist's estate, she has to do something to manage the tax ramifications, and she needs professional advice from advisors who work with a team of experts.

As a practical matter, the Disclaimer Trust should only be used if Nora has sufficient business acumen, and expert financial advice, to help make certain her choices on accepting or disclaiming property are the right ones for her and her family. She should seek the advice of an attorney.

Also, if Dr. Dentist has any concern that Nora's shopping habits may tempt her into accepting his entire estate into her own, and disclaiming none of the assets regardless of the tax results, then the Disclaimer Trust is a bad idea in that situation.

In the case of Dr. Dentist, a Disclaimer Trust would be a smart tool for their estate plan. But for Walt the plumber, he would certainly not need Wife #3 deciding which of his assets should go into her Survivor's Trust. Walt's goals would be better met by putting his separate property into a Bypass Trust with his children as beneficiaries, along with Wife #3, as well as a QTIP Trust to assure an inheritance for his children.

Family Pot Trust –with Sprinkling Powers or "Sprinkling Trust"

A good tool for a family with minor children, like Dr. Dentist and Nora, is the Family Pot Trust. This trust pools together property for the benefit of their children into a single trust, as opposed to funding two separate trusts.

If the trustee is given "sprinkling power" over the distribution of trust assets, it means the trustee has full discretion to decide when to pay money, how much to pay, and what proportion of the trust to pay to each child.

The effect of allowing a trustee to "sprinkle" income and principal between the children is to substitute the same discretion as a parent. In this fashion, if both parents are deceased, the trustee has the power to provide for unforeseen crisis, or medical attention, or any other emergency.

The kind of flexibility provided in the "sprinkling power" allows the trustee to respond to the different needs of the children as they arise.

Otherwise, the trustee is limited to distributions of money to each child based on rigid trust formulas, or rules limiting distribution only from specific income property, or only at a specific time. The Family Pot Trust is thought to be a more equitable method of distributing income to children.

Your children may all be loved the same, but they each have their own interest and ambitions, as well as health and emergency financial needs. These needs require that various amounts of money be expended.

A Family Pot Trust assures equal response to each child's unequal emergency needs, but it will make life difficult for the trustee who decides which child's emergency is more important.

A Sprinkling Trust "in three stages" is a Family Pot Trust which begins to terminate when the youngest child has turned 18 or 20. In the case of two daughters, they would each receive an equal share portion of the trust as soon as the youngest turned 18.

A second sum may be distributed to each of them when the youngest turns 26, and the third and final portion of the trust would be distributed to both daughters when the youngest reached age 30. However, the distribution ages are totally up to the parents.

Generation Skipping Trust

Do not confuse the "generation-skipping tax," with the "federal estate and gift tax." The "federal estate tax and gift tax" is a *unified* tax. The estate and gift tax draw from the same tax exemption.

To avoid paying the estate tax, you use the marital deduction exemption, and to avoid paying taxes on an annual gift to your child, you use the annual gift tax exemption. (See *How The Federal Tax Exemption Works in Chapter Ten.*)

For example, if you died in the year 2008 your estate could exempt up to $2 million and not pay any estate taxes. This is scheduled to drop to only $1 million in 2011. (See chart on page 111.)

During your lifetime, if you had made two annual gifts of $50,000 each, each gift would have been $38,000 in excess of the annual gift tax deduction of $12,000 (you get an $12,000 deduction each year regardless of any more money you gift); and you took the tax credit of $50,000 for each of the years you made the gifts.

Then your "marital deduction exemption" of $2 million would have been reduced by the total of $76,000 for both the gifts, to $1,924,000. ($2 million reduced by 2 years X a $38,000 overage of the $12,000 gift exemption, allowed each year since 2006.)

The "generation-skipping tax" is a horse of a different color. It is only in very large estates where generation-skipping trusts are necessary to avoid paying the "federal generation-skipping transfer tax."

This is when tools such as the "reverse QTIP Trust" can be used to obtain an "inclusion ratio of zero" (no tax) so you won't pay any taxes on the transfer. This goal is based entirely on the size of an individual's wealth, their expert tax representation, and personal desires.

Providing for Your Grandchildren

Generation-skipping tax planning is usually for families who want to transfer their wealth tax-free to children for generations to come. Generation-skipping means leaving a portion of your wealth for the third generation, such as if Walt the plumber wanted to leave special assets for his grandchildren.

But Walt's estate is probably not large enough to worry about generation skipping, unless it is a priority for him. His desired results can be achieved by using other estate planning tools, while leaving his primary wealth to his second generation.

In extremely large estates, separate third generation-skipping trusts can be funded for each grandchild so each grandchild's share is so large it far exceeds all normally anticipated needs for their formative years. This is when there truly is enough money to go around.

This would not be Walt's concern. He has four adult children and a wife with whom to share his estate. He can provide for his grandchildren by first providing for his children, whose share will, should they die before Walt, go to that child's children.

Beyond the issue of wealth, a parent's desire to incur the complexities involved in a third generation trust is dependent upon their relationship with their grandchildren. The closer the relationship, the more inclined they are to incur the complexities.

Tax considerations play a part in, but do not rule, the decision making process. Most grandparents usually do not feel obliged to support their grandchildren. A parent's primary concern is most often protecting their own children from squandering their inheritance at an early age, thus the name Spendthrift Trust.

CHAPTER SIXTEEN

Practical Trusts, Beginning with the CRUT

The "**Charitable Remainder Unitrust**" is a gift from the government that rewards your philanthropy. You give to the charity of your choice when you die, and the government gives you your tax dollars while you live. It trades charity for tax dollars.

There is no trust more giving, or more receiving, than the charitable remainder unitrust. It has flexible terms and conditions, and is adaptable to any taxpayer with a highly appreciated asset and a very low cost basis.

For example, a rental property purchased for $200,000, which is now worth $1 million, or a stock share that is presently worth $100, but was purchased for $2.00, are the types of highly appreciated assets that make a good corpus for a trust. In other words, wherever there is an enormous capital gains tax looming, there is a need for a charitable remainder unitrust.

The charitable remainder unitrust (CRUT) is an irrevocable trust that defers your donation to charity, gives you the immediate benefit of the tax deduction, and a specified sum of money paid annually, quarterly or monthly until the "remainder" becomes due. The best way to describe the benefits of a CRUT is to give an example of how it works.

Assume that a 65 year-old gentleman named Fritz has a stock portfolio worth $600,000. Fritz purchased these stocks back in the '70's for $5,000. If he sold the stock today, he would pay capital gains tax on $595,000 at the 15% federal rate, and 9.3% for the California state capital gains tax. That would be $144,585 in taxes.

Because of this huge tax consequence, rather than sell his stocks Fritz has been living off the margin of his stock account. This means he has been borrowing money against the value of his stocks from his brokerage firm at a rate of about 8% interest. Paying 8% interest on the borrowed income is better than paying the 24.3% state and federal capital gains tax he would be required to pay if he sold the stocks. After all, the stocks continue to increase in value and make him money.

Many older people in Fritz's position live off the margin of their securities account. If they are old enough they simply outlive the amount of money they can borrow on the account. It is a good strategy if all the numbers work out right. It is a very poor strategy if you run beyond your margin restraint (which is the amount of money you are allowed to borrow before the brokerage house calls for it to be paid off) while you are still alive.

This way there is never a taxable event to gouge their estate of their much needed funds for living. When they die, the margin account dies with them and they never have to pay taxes on their much appreciated stock profit they have been using for living expenses. That's one way to save.

But Fritz is not that old, or that rich. His margin account is now maxed out at $100,000, and the brokerage house is demanding payment.

In order to pay back the $100,000 loan, Fritz has to sell nearly $135,000 worth of stock. This is because $32,805 of that sale would go to federal and state taxes. To get $100,000 Fritz has to pay $32,805 more in taxes. That is a bad deal.

However, because Fritz is 65 years old, a smart alternative would be for him to donate the $135,000 to his favorite charity, the "Fiesta Foundation," through a charitable remainder unitrust. This CRUT will pay Fritz 5% of the CRUT's value every year for life. More importantly, the contribution will create an income tax deduction in the year of contribution of $63,107 (according to the IRS tables and interest rates of January, 2006).

Using this tax deduction, Fritz would only need to sell $111,843 in securities (not $135,000) to have $100,000 left after taxes to pay the margin loan. Using the tax benefit of the CRUT, he is able to pay off the margin loan at a cost of $11,843 in taxes vs. $32,805 in taxes.

Referring to the CRUT's immediate "tax benefit" or "tax credit" can be misleading in the sense that the contribution to the CRUT does not provide a "dollar for dollar" reduction in tax. The contribution of the property to the CRUT provides a tax deduction toward "computing" taxable income, and therefore, the income tax is lower. (The exact tax credit is determined by a complicated IRS formula, crossing age and life expectancy with valuation tables, interest rate, etc.)

To eliminate taxes entirely on selling his stock to pay off the margin, Fritz would have to contribute $214,000 to the CRUT. This would provide a $100,000 tax deduction (instead of the $63,107 tax deduction above) enabling $100,000 of his securities to be sold to pay off the margin loan. (Again, refer to your CPA's IRS tax tables.)

At the end of the year, Fritz will have paid off his margin account, have $214,000 in his CRUT, and will have paid NO TAXES on the appreciated and/or sold stocks in the CRUT. However, Fritz, or any other recipient of the CRUT distribution funds, is taxed as personal income on the money they receive from the CRUT.

Fritz will be the sole beneficiary of the CRUT for life, and he will receive quarterly payments from the CRUT to supplement his other earned income. The stocks in the CRUT can continue to appreciate at a meteoric rate, and there will never be any income tax to pay on the capital gains until they are distributed. All CRUT gains are income tax exempt!

Now comes the best part. As sole beneficiary to the CRUT, Fritz is entitled to a specified percentage of at least 5% of the net market value of the CRUT, each year for life.

There is some flexibility in the distribution percentage of this yearly sum because, like the tax benefit above, the exact amount of money Fritz will be paid is determined by a formula on an IRS software program.

However, when the trust is terminated, such as when Fritz dies, and the donation to the charity (termed the "remainder") becomes due, the minimum net amount of trust assets that goes to the "Fiesta Foundation" is ten percent; and in some cases only five percent.

Ten percent of $214,000 is $21,400. That is a good deal for both Fritz and the Fiesta Foundation. Meanwhile, the stock in the CRUT may appreciate two or three times over, if Fritz is very, very lucky.

By examining the benefits that Fritz received from the CRUT, you can extrapolate on how those benefits might apply to your own financial legacy. The CRUT, as a deferred giving tool, can be very versatile and serve many purposes when used with a little imagination.

As another example, if husband (and of course vice versa) wants to provide for the security of wife, he could put that $2 million piece of appreciated property he has been holding into a Charitable Remainder Unitrust and sell it tax-free. Over the next twenty years the CRUT could pay out $90,000 (or more or less) a year to wife for her sole benefit from the $2 million sale. Also, the $2 million that goes into the CRUT is deducted from the gross value of their estate. Therefore, it is not counted for estate tax purposes at death, as long as the trust terminates at death. However, if there is a successor trustee (one who follows the first, or second,etc.) then only a portion of the CRUT is excluded.

In deciding whether or not to use a CRUT, just add the tax advantages, along with the life time benefits, and the benefit to your charity. It may help you sleep at night. For many people, it is the best option for the family, and for posterity at the same time.

College Savings Trusts

Another example of a charitable remainder trust is an "annuity trust." This charitable remainder "trust" is different from the "unitrust" because it provides a specific amount of money to the beneficiary for a specific amount of time – like money to your daughter during her four (five?) years in college.

Let us assume Fritz has a daughter named Debby who is about to enter college. He wants to do something *smart* to help pay for her education, and something *good* for his favorite charity.

Fritz decides to take $100,000 of stock from his brokerage account in the same year Debby is starting college, and puts it in a Charitable Remainder Trust (CRT).

In the CRT, the stocks can appreciate, or be liquidated, without creating a taxable event, just like the CRUT, and the funds in the trust are tax exempt. Fritz has also avoided the capital gains tax he would otherwise have paid had he simply sold the stocks to pay for Debby's education.

Fritz decides to use a five-year term for the annuity trust to make payouts to Debby (by the end of college, she calls herself Deborah). At the specified percentage rate of 18% per year, Deborah will receive $18,000 (or a little less each year as the trust value diminishes) while in college, and one year after college. One *caveat*, the $18,000 is taxable income to Deborah, but her tax bracket should be relatively low.

That totals a sum of $90,000 to Deborah, and if the trust averages 8% interest per year, Fritz's favorite trust, the "Fiesta Foundation" will receive approximately $50,000 after five years.

That is a win, win, win situation, for Deborah, Fritz *and* the Fiesta Foundation.

Something to always remember when planning for your children's college education is that the assets that fund the Charitable Remainder Trust are income tax exempt. That means the original $100,000 asset can be sold and reinvested, and bought and diversified and sold again and again without any tax ramifications.

This makes it much easier to accumulate wealth. Therefore, if Debby's CRT is started when she is five, there are thirteen years to build her college fund. The ten percent that must remain in the trust for charity only applies to the original net value of the trust. The rest of the value in the trust is accumulated wealth.

The 529 Plan, State Agencies Provide College Savings

When considering college savings plans it is well worth mentioning a "529 Plan." In California this state-run savings program is called the "ScholarShare Trust." It is administered by a state agency called the "ScholarShare Investment Board," which began accepting investments in 1999.

Similar to programs in other states, the purpose of this trust is to help people save money for college. Saving is encouraged by the plan's enhanced state and federal tax benefits, and is as easy as opening a bank account for your child, niece, nephew, or a friend.

The ScholarShare Trust is a "hands off" investment for contributors and is managed by a professional investment firm for a .8% fee. The 529 Plan's best feature is that the earned income from the savings is tax exempt. When the funds are distributed, for college use only, the student will not pay any income tax on the earned income produced by the investment plan, although he will pay taxes on the money he receives as earned income.

Contributing to California's 529 Plan is the same as opening a savings account with the "Golden State" and you can do so with as little as $25.00. There are various investment plans to choose from, but the investment is not federally insured and can fluctuate with the market.

As with any gift plan, you can contribute up to $12,000 each year without having to file a gift tax return, and can contribute up to $285,000 overall in California. You can "front load" up to 5 years, but you can only fund 529 plans with cash. Some of the investment options are guaranteed, and some are not. It is highly advisable you check with a tax advisor before contributing to a 529 Plan. For more information go to:

www.ScholarShare.com, or
www.SavingForCollege.com

Recently a client had wanted to set up seven different trusts, for seven different nieces and nephews, in several different states. Once she realized the cost to establish seven trusts, along paying a trustee to administer each trust, she began to rethink her plan. Because she was adamant the beneficiaries were to use the money only for "higher" education, meaning above high school, she realized the expense was far beyond her means, let alone the ability to find seven trustees to invest the individual trust funds wisely, and then to distribute the funds as directed. Complicating matters for the formation of the trusts were the different laws governing trusts in the different states where her nieces and nephews were living. It was beginning to look like an impossible dream.

Because of that, she decided she would place the funds for each child in California's ScholarShare plan, and if not used by the beneficiary for educational purposes, regardless of the state they were in, the remainder would go to another person she specified as a beneficiary.

That was a very smart decision on her part and saved thousands of dollars on individual trusts, and priceless peace of mind knowing the money would be spent only for educational purposes.

Family Wealth Transfers Through Business Entities

a. Using FLPs and LLCs

"Family Limited Partnerships" (FLP) and "Limited Liability Companies" (LLC) are legal entities older family members can use to transfer ownership of wealth to younger family members while gaining enhanced tax savings.

But if you ever wanted to get paranoid about the IRS and their recent move to uncover FLPs and LLCs as vehicles for fraudulent transfers, just spend a day with an IRS tax attorney, and let him count the ways of tearing apart an FLP to make certain it has a specific and meaningful business purpose.

These transfers are usually suspect when donors retain too much management and control over the assets, or coincidentally transfer and sell their assets into one of these entities immediately before death.

When the guilty get busted, the assets are transferred back into the donor's estate and the participants are penalized under IRC §§ 2038, 2036, and the newly developed IRS Circular 230 - all of which are way beyond the scope of this book. The penalty is normally 20% of the gross value on the property you attempted to give away to **evade** taxes.

Much of the controversy centers on "valuation discounts" and whether the transaction's "principle purpose" is tax avoidance, or whether its "significant purpose" is tax avoidance. Catch the difference between "principle" and "significant" avoidance?

In simple language, you cannot put your house or business in a partnership just to transfer a "minor interest" in ownership to your children so you can avoid taxes. There must be a legitimate business reason for creating the business entity; like an actual business that was established years before the death, and was done so to actually make money.

As a point of relative interest, IRS Reg. 230 is directly related to the "disclaimer" boldly set forth in the front of this book. The disclaimer assures the reader that no opinion herein is a "marketed opinion," and no information provided can be used to avoid tax penalties for which the taxpayer would otherwise be responsible.

This disclaimer is necessary to make sure some knucklehead doesn't get into trouble with the IRS and then blame the author of this material for giving him illegal tax advice. The standard taxpayer's excuse for cheating on his/her taxes is, "I reasonably relied on my professional." Once again, in case you missed it the first time, the difference between tax avoidance and tax evasion is as follows:

The city you live in has a toll bridge that will get you home one-half hour earlier than if you drive five miles out of your way to take the free bridge. If you take the free bridge you are **avoiding** taxes, which is perfectly legal. But, if you attempt to crash through the toll bridge to get home, you are attempting to **evade** taxes, and you will be sharing a cell with Al Capone.

For the sake of general knowledge, an FLP, disparagingly referred to by the IRS as a "vanilla flip," is a Family Limited Partnership where investors hold partnership shares, and a LLC is a Limited Liability Company where investors hold membership shares.

They are both legal entities into which you can transfer wealth such as a business interest, stocks, real estate holdings, etc., and they both provide creditor protection for legitimate business purposes.

The primary objective of all estate planning is to preserve and transfer wealth from one generation to the next, with the least possible transfer cost, i.e. taxes, before and/or after death.

In the mid 1980's, the "tax shelter industry" began to remove assets from their client's large estates and transfer them into a FLP or LLC where both the parents and their children were investors.

For starters, this reduces the size of the parents' estate for estate tax purposes. It also allows for the value of the assets to be transferred to younger family members with the tax advantage of greatly reducing their value, both through the manipulation of "valuation discounts" and "liquidation rights."

Do not be concerned with these discounts and rights, unless you are very serious about transferring large amounts of stock, realty or business shares to your children while you are alive.

To take proper advantage of these opportunities, you need a good tax attorney, a CPA, and an "expert" appraiser to determine discounts for lack of control, lack of marketability for "fractional interests" in real property, and for interests in business entities (FLPs, LLCs) which hold traditional and non-traditional assets.

b. If The Above Sounds Like Gobbledygook, Read This

Please heed this advice: if you enter into an LLC you must make certain that the managing members' duties and liabilities are specifically stated in the operative agreement. You must make sure the managing members are not given any powers beyond the limitations restricting those activities. You should never allow the managers (usually one or two members) to overrule the financial majority of the other contributing members. You should be very careful that the managing member's powers do not include broadening their powers over you. All states may be different, but this is one precaution that is universal.

The use of different business entities to transfer appreciated property between family members has increasingly become more commonplace, and in many cases fundamental to estate planning. As explained below, in transferring my own real estate interest to my daughter, I use an LLC in my estate plan. I can do this because I have a legitimate real estate business, of which I am the broker, that I have run, along with my law practice, for about ten years.

There are many forms of business entities to choose from when parents want to move their commercial property or family business into a form of co-ownership with their children. As older family members give ownership to younger family members, they receive what are called "valuation discounts" on the property. These discounts are determined by expert appraisers, and it can save them tax dollars.

Consider a situation where a Mom and Dad have a six-plex apartment house they purchased ten years ago for $200,000, now worth $1 million. Junior and Sis' are 18 and 19 years old. Mom and Dad want to introduce them to the world of apartment management, and help develop their business acumen.

They want to do it gradually by transferring control and ownership management over the years. They also want to reduce the tax liability of transferring ownership, as opposed to outright gifting it to their children.

These are some of their business entity options:

1. Tenancy in common. Each family member owns a piece of the whole, but the ownership interest is cumbersome and it is difficult to establish ownership transfers. Because of the restrictions of ownership for tenants in common, it does not allow "minority interest" (Junior and Sis's interest) to do what they want with the property. This can result in family litigation, such as a right to partition, which could lead to a "cloud on the title," let alone a cloud on the family.

2. Trusts. While there are many types of trusts to choose from, they are not always the best choices. Each one brings with it the duty of fiduciary powers and special tax considerations. Also, each trust has regulations regarding the beneficiaries, and that may not allow for the desired freedom that was intended.

3. Corporations. A corporation must follow strict regulations, but more importantly this entity is inflexible in getting funds out of the corporation. Donors (Mom and Dad) are also subject to double taxation where, for example, they transfer their car to the corporation and have to pay tax on its use, or where they sell highly-appreciated assets through the corporation, and then have to pay both corporate and personal income tax.

4. General Partnership or Joint Venture. These partnerships are convenient, but offer nothing in terms of tax advantages or credit protection.

5. Limited Partnership vs. Limited Liability Company. The "Limited Partnership" was once the preferred business entity for owning family property, or a business. It still is popular where there is a preferred distinction between two classes of investors. (The California Uniform Limited Partnership Act of 2008 considerably changes the law preceding this recent Act.)

The difference between a Limited Partnership and an LLC is that an LP *always* has two tiers of partnership interests. There are the limited partners and the general partners. The limited partners have no hand in management, and the general partners are the managers of the business enterprise.

Therefore, the general partners can be held personally liable for the negligent acts or business failures of the organization, and the limited partners cannot.

Because of this vulnerability of personal liability, general partners were often cloaked in the protection of a corporate entity. That meant it was not Mom and Dad who were the general partners of the partnership, but Mom and Dad, Inc., a Delaware corporation.

This way, it was Mom and Dad's corporate identity that was open to direct liability from creditors, and their personal assets remained safely "veiled" behind the corporate structure, as long as they followed all the corporate rules.

As clever a relationship as this was, it created problems to have multiple entities as part of the same partnership, not the least of which was accounting for the corporate and partnership income.

The LLC is now the preferred business entity in California for holding real property or a family business. Investors are called "members." Unless the articles of organization of the LLC state otherwise, the business affairs of the company are "member managed," and there are no separate classes of investors.

This allows for great flexibility in management. It can be as decentralized, democratic or informal as a general partnership; it can adopt a corporate style of management, with a board of directors and managers; or alternatively, it can adopt a management style analogous to a limited partnership. It all depends on how the articles of organization are written.

The best feature is members of an LLC are not personally liable for the debts, obligation, or liabilities of the LLC. Mom, Dad, Junior, and Sis' all have limited liability. This limited liability protects members regardless of whether the liability arises in contract, tort or otherwise. However, if the family home or vacation rentals are assets of the LLC, then it would defeat the limited liability protection, unless adequately insured.

However, there are exceptions to this rule and members may be held personally liable if a court "pierces the company veil" of the LLC. This is similar to "piercing the corporate veil" but the court does not consider the failure to hold member or manager meetings, or the failure to observe other formalities required in the Operating Agreement because hopefully, your attorney did not put such formalities in your Operating Agreement.

As for transferring financial interest, the LLC member can transfer their financial interest without the consent of others. Therefore, when Junior gets older and wants to cash out to become a rock star, he can sell his membership interest to another person. But as it is with all partnerships, he can only sell his interest in the right to the distribution of profit or loss, not voting or management rights -- although that may be of little consolation to Mom and Dad.

The LLC is also attractive because of the pass-through tax treatment to the members. It avoids the double taxation issue of a corporation. The downside in California is an LLC, as well as an FLP, is subject to an annual tax of $800.

CHAPTER SEVENTEEN

Who Makes Up These Laws?

Gambling your life expectancy against the IRS actuary tables just to get a huge tax break is the type of legal strategy that really makes you wonder who writes these tax avoidance tools into law.

Feeling lucky? Here is a legitimate way to put your residence into a trust, then transfer ownership to your children and earn a great tax advantage for yourself - providing you live long enough.

It is called a Qualified Personal Residence Trust (QPRT). The IRS allows you to bet that you will outlive their actuary tables. Say you are 60 years old. You put your residence (or vacation home) in an irrevocable trust naming your children as final beneficiaries after a term of your choice, say 15 years.

If you live long enough to see your children own your house, you not only get full ownership rights to your house for those 15 years, but a big reduction by the IRS on the gift tax, *and* the residence is not included in your estate tax upon your death! At the end of the 15 year term, the transaction typically results in a "leaseback" to the transferor. These lease payments will further decrease the size of the transferor's estate.

The term of the trust is up to you, but the older you are, and the longer the term of the trust, the bigger the IRS tax credit.

If you do not outlive the 15 year term of the trust, the residence is added back into your estate and there is no added benefit. It is simply a lost opportunity and you are out the money for the formation of the trust.

The QPRT is actually a good deal, but it has to be done for the right reasons. Those reasons include:

- A desire to see your children enjoy your house;
- To help develop your heirs' asset base;
- To provide needed support to your children while relieving your own financial burden; and/or
- To protect assets from your or your children's creditors.

There are many other reasons to gift your assets to your heirs, but tax reduction should not be the main one. Too many things can go wrong between the gifting and the afterlife.

Many of us who are between the ages of 45 and 65 have children who believe they have a right of entitlement to everything their parents have, and they want it now. The law books are filled with cases of children suing their parents for their share of the "partnership," because they do not want to wait for their inheritance.

If your children are not like that, great, but it is something of a national epidemic. Children in their 30's and 40's are moving back home. Be careful if you choose a QPRT. Unfortunately, you will never know, until it's too late, if you can trust your children, but mainly because the trust is irrevocable. Once it is done, it cannot be undone.

For those who would like it illustrated for them, in 1982, after passing the bar, I went to work in an office where there was a much older and respected attorney. He had this happen to him. His name was Richard and he always did his own taxes. He presented himself as having the expertise of a tax specialist, but while I doubt he was certified, he certainly had the experience.

He was an intimidating attorney and he worked constantly changing various aspects of his estate plan. It included two daughters by a previous marriage, and his very lovely, active and friendly wife. He was a multi-millionaire, and as part of the estate plan, he transferred ownership interest in several of his properties to his daughters while he was still alive, with the remainder to go to them after he was gone. Unfortunately, they did not want to wait for their inheritance.

Whatever their interest may have been, and whether it was a QPRT or not, makes no difference. The point is, because they had an ownership interest in the properties, they had the right to sue their father on whatever creative breach or tort an attorney could dream up regarding an interference with their prospective business advantage. And that is exactly what they did, despite the lack of legal credence. As a result, Richard was in litigation against his two daughters for the next two years before his heart was finally broken enough to give in to the emotional stress. He signed over his remaining interest in the properties to his daughters, and they never spoke again for the rest of his life.

For that reason, the QPRT, and its cousins the GRAT and the GRIT, are recommended only to those parents, or single people who feel comfortable their heirs are reasonable, and who have sought reliable tax advice, and who have enough assets, just in case things go south.

If you believe your estate will be within the allotted tax exemption limit when you, or both you and your spouse die, then there is no need to consider a QPRT.

What kind of mind thought up a new tax deduction that would stop your house or vacation home from being added to the value of your estate for tax purposes, *only* if you irrevocably promised to leave the house to your descendants, and you outlived a specified term of years? Do IRS agents make bets on whether you'll outlive the term of years, either set by yourself, or set by your probable lifetime according to the IRS actuary tables? The answer is, of course not. The QPRT is actually a gift from the IRS. The only catch is, to get the gift deduction you must outlive the term of years, or the actuary death date. If you fail, all that happens is you get nothing. The house is simply transferred back into your estate after your death and taxed on.

Of course your gift deduction would be greatly reduced if you chose a term of years rather then challenge the actuary tables, but that is not the actual advantage of the tax tool for normal Baby Boomers. In fact, the law is not for "normal" Baby Boomers.

First, you should have two homes. If you put your summer home, or your residence, into a QPRT at age 70, when the IRS actuary table states your life term is 78 years old, and you chose the option of outliving the actuary table, you could only get the gift tax deduction if you lived to be 79 years old -- otherwise you get nothing.

Of course it does not stop there, that is only one thing to consider. The gifting of the house may be a gift deduction for the donor, but the donee must pay tax on the earned income from the property, and that makes a big difference if the donee is in the 35% tax bracket instead of the

23% tax bracket. And what if the house gains little value and you live to be 90 years old? Would it have been better to hold on to the house, and have the children pay the estate tax? What if your estate value falls below the marital tax exemption? What difference would it make then?

This is not why this tax was devised. It was devised for the very wealthy, perhaps the top 2% of the population. Somebody had to pay a clever tax attorney, or building full of tax attorneys, and congressmen, who created this Code by using tax implication from the IRS Code and Regs, as well as any tax opinions from the Federal Appellate Courts from across the nation, to set a precedent for the IRS to allow such a novel gamble as a QPRT as a tax tool.

How this gamble really works is no gamble at all. They richer Baby Boomers have plenty of assets and different homes, and they sure as heck are not going to choose a period of years they are not certain to live past just to get that deduction. Putting aside a fatal accident (in which case they probably have triple indemnity insurance), they are the ones who are going to benefit from this tool.

As explained in Chapter Ten, this is just another vehicle for the wealthy to pass on their assets, with no transfer tax, to their children, grandchildren, and even "ancestors" who are included in the list of eligible donees for a QPRT.

If the vacation home is worth $4 million, a QPRT saves $1,800,000 in estate taxes by not having the "vacation home" added back into a $2 million estate in 2008. Why? Because it would otherwise be $4 million above the marital tax exemption and be taxed at 45%.

There are, of course, strict rules in order for a house to qualify for a QPRT, so that is why they have the GRIT and GRAT and some other acronyms, which you can learn about when you get to that stage. If you ever picked up a horn-book, or learned treatise on the subject, you immediately became aware that there are so many pitfalls which may or may not occur, and what might be great for one part of your estate plan could make another part a disaster.

Again, this is why you want a law firm to either do it right, or to be held responsible if they do not. That is why attorneys carry malpractice insurance. Some of the documents are so long and complicated and integrated, it takes time to make sure they are right. Most people do not want to pay for that time, so the documents are not checked, rechecked, and then checked again, to make certain all the ends tie together. It is a big job, but isn't 50 years of your life's work worth making sure the job is done right?

CHAPTER EIGHTEEN

Estate Planning For Pets

Believe it or not, this is a very sophisticated trust, and difficult to make legally binding. It takes specialized expertise because most states do not recognize any trust where the beneficiary is an animal. This means a "Pet Trust" must be worded in a way the pet itself is not the beneficiary, since an animal cannot enforce its rights in court, like a trustee or caregiver could. That causes an attorney in most states to customize the trust to specific situations to keep it within the bounds of the law. This normally makes a "Pet Trust" another benefit for those rich enough to pay for this legal skill.

Otherwise, the trust will not be recognized by the court and all your efforts will be in vain. Another factor is the recommendation that such a trust be funded with a minimum of $10,000 to $50,000 per animal. That adds up for your dog, your cat, or your pony.

I love my dog as much as you love yours, and it is usually thought of as a last minute consideration as to who will care for the dog. But many people do not get that last minute and they want to be certain the dog, cat, horse or plural of each, does not end up in the pound or glue factory. Some people are obsessive, and borderline insane, when it comes to caring for their pet after they cannot do it themselves anymore. This includes people who become disabled.

I am sure you will not find it hard to believe California is the only state in the nation to solve this pet issue pursuant to law. California has developed what is called an "Honorary Trust" under California Probate Code § 15212. It is called a "Companion Animal Trust" to assure their pet or pets are provided for exactly the way they want after they are gone. When the pet dies, the trust terminates, so it must determine where the remainder of the trust money goes, and that can be tricky.

It may seem strange someone may go to the expense of providing for their beloved pet in this grand fashion, but there are plenty of clients who do, and there is a lot to be learned from how the Companion Animal Trust works because it ties together much of what has been discussed in this book.

First of all, it is a separate trust that is provided in the same way a Bypass Trust is established after the death of the first spouse in a joint revocable trust. The difference is this Revocable Trust is called a Companion Animal Trust, the same as you have a Durable Power of Attorney, Revocable Trust or a Will.

One difference is the Companion Animal Trust could be put in place **after** the first spouse or partner (you do not have to be married to take advantage) has died. The surviving spouse or partner could create the Companion Animal Trust from her or his Survivor's Trust.

The Companion Animal Trust can have the pet as the beneficiary, but there is also normally a caretaker to manage the pet, and a trustee to handle the expenses. Such expenses may include paying the caretaker, as well as paying the veterinary bills. It must be determined beforehand, who has the right to choose the veterinarian, the caretaker or the trustee?

Under the law providing for this Companion Animal Trust, Probate Code 15212 provides that a trust for the care of a designated domestic or pet animal "may be performed by the trustee for the life of the animal, whether or not there is a beneficiary who can seek enforcement or termination of the trust, and whether or not the terms of the trust contemplate a longer duration.'

In other words, the trust terminates upon the death of the pet, but until then, the trustee is responsible for managing the trust, unless (although it does not say this) a caretaker was also named as a co-trustee. That is where the fancy maneuvering comes in. After the pet's death, the remainder of the money is distributed outright to the remainder beneficiary. Therefore, whoever you name as trustee, or caregiver, better have the best interest of the animal in mind. This is particularly true if you also make them the remainder beneficiary. In this case they get all that is left when the pet dies. If there is $12 million in the trust to take care of a French poodle, as was recently widespread about Leona Helmsley's dog, and you were the beneficiary of the money that remained after the dog's death, you would certainly hope you outlived the dog.

This is why some clever thinking must be worded into the trust agreement, just like a Bypass Trust agreement, as to whom, how, when and to what extent the trustee may act, as well as exactly what your expectation is of your pet's care while alive, and how the remainder is to be distributed to a specific beneficiary.

As for the remainder beneficiary, you might want to leave the money for the college education of young nieces or nephews. But a better approach to eliminating any outside pressure might be to leave the remaining money to charity. Afterall, this is your pet trust, not your family estate plan. Ask yourself, what would George Washington do? He was big on charity too.

CHAPTER NINETEEN

Reexamining Estate Plans

Now that everything has been covered from "Transmutation Agreements," to "Disclaimer Trust," to "Limited Liability Companies," it is time to reexamine the flow charts depicting the estate strategies of Dr. Dentist and Walt the Plumber. Starting with the two basic plans, look at the follow up pages that show the types of notes or charts you should be writing to determine your own strategy.

All of the flow charts in this book can be found in chronological order in the Appendix to give you a feel for the entire web of estate planning ideas. If you take the time to study them, and reflect on the strengths and weaknesses of each scenario, you will begin to feel like you know what you are talking about. As soon as that happens, you are ready to talk with an attorney and begin your own estate planning.

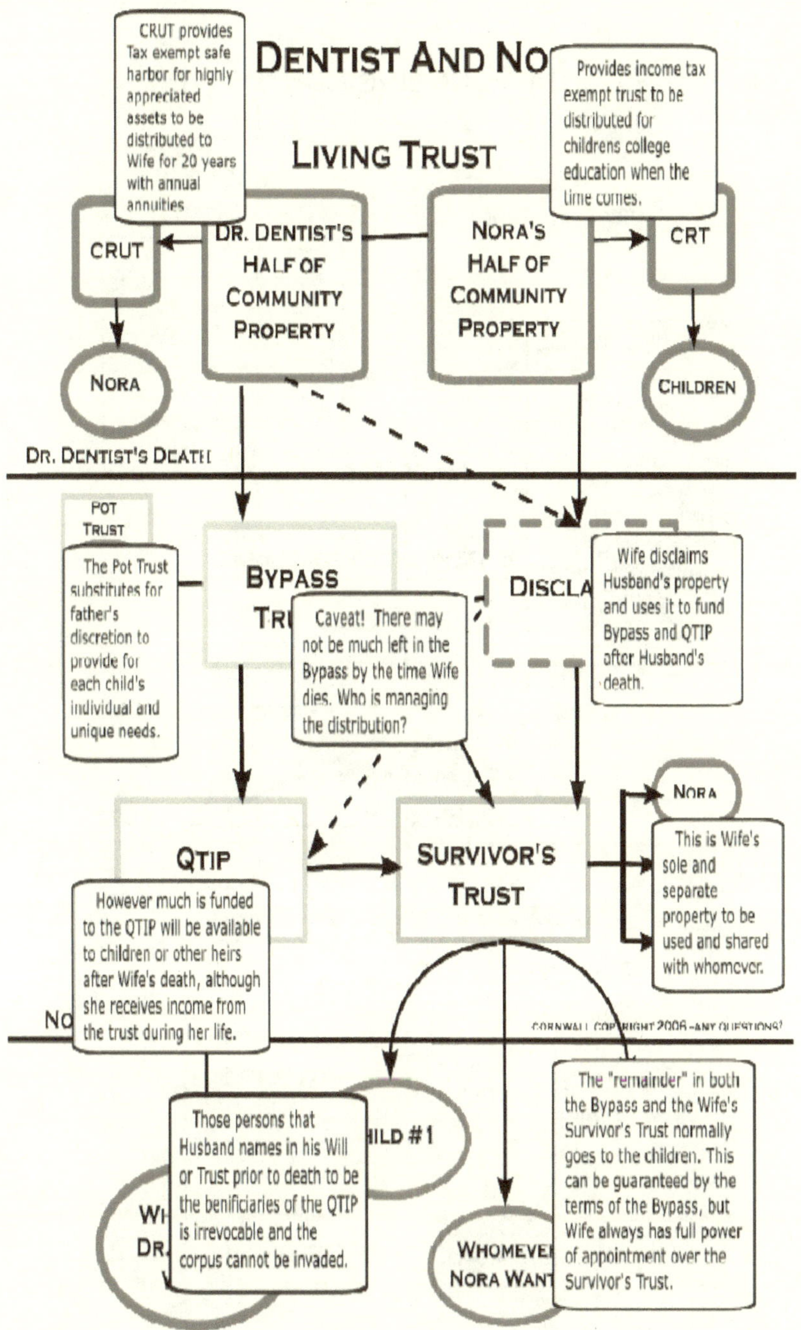
DENTIST AND NO
LIVING TRUST
CRUT provides Tax exempt safe harbor for highly appreciated assets to be distributed to Wife for 20 years with annual annuities
Provides income tax exempt trust to be distributed for childrens college education when the time comes.
CRUT
DR. DENTIST'S HALF OF COMMUNITY PROPERTY
NORA'S HALF OF COMMUNITY PROPERTY
CRT
NORA
CHILDREN
DR. DENTIST'S DEATH
POT TRUST
The Pot Trust substitutes for father's discretion to provide for each child's individual and unique needs.
BYPASS TRU
Caveat! There may not be much left in the Bypass by the time Wife dies. Who is managing the distribution?
DISCLA
Wife disclaims Husband's property and uses it to fund Bypass and QTIP after Husband's death.
QTIP
SURVIVOR'S TRUST
NORA
This is Wife's sole and separate property to be used and shared with whomever.
However much is funded to the QTIP will be available to children or other heirs after Wife's death, although she receives income from the trust during her life.
NO
CORNWALL COPYRIGHT 2006 - ANY QUESTIONS?
HILD #1
Those persons that Husband names in his Will or Trust prior to death to be the benificiaries of the QTIP is irrevocable and the corpus cannot be invaded.
WH
DR.
WHOMEVE
NORA WANT
The "remainder" in both the Bypass and the Wife's Survivor's Trust normally goes to the children. This can be guaranteed by the terms of the Bypass, but Wife always has full power of appointment over the Survivor's Trust.

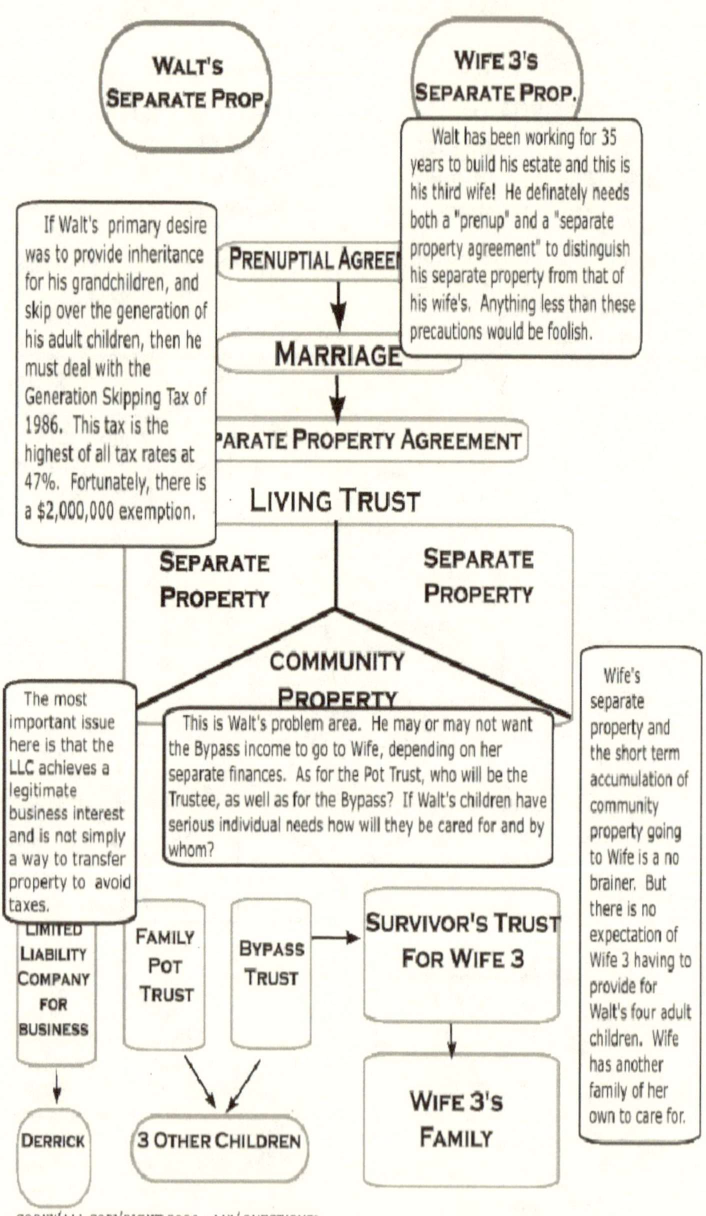
WALT THE PLUMBING CONTRACTOR
WALT'S SEPARATE PROP.
WIFE 3'S SEPARATE PROP.
Walt has been working for 35 years to build his estate and this is his third wife! He definately needs both a "prenup" and a "separate property agreement" to distinguish his separate property from that of his wife's. Anything less than these precautions would be foolish.
If Walt's primary desire was to provide inheritance for his grandchildren, and skip over the generation of his adult children, then he must deal with the Generation Skipping Tax of 1986. This tax is the highest of all tax rates at 47%. Fortunately, there is a $2,000,000 exemption.
PRENUPTIAL AGREE
MARRIAGE
PARATE PROPERTY AGREEMENT
LIVING TRUST
SEPARATE PROPERTY
SEPARATE PROPERTY
COMMUNITY PROPERTY
Wife's separate property and the short term accumulation of community property going to Wife is a no brainer. But there is no expectation of Wife 3 having to provide for Walt's four adult children. Wife has another family of her own to care for.
The most important issue here is that the LLC achieves a legitimate business interest and is not simply a way to transfer property to avoid taxes.
This is Walt's problem area. He may or may not want the Bypass income to go to Wife, depending on her separate finances. As for the Pot Trust, who will be the Trustee, as well as for the Bypass? If Walt's children have serious individual needs how will they be cared for and by whom?
LIMITED LIABILITY COMPANY FOR BUSINESS
FAMILY POT TRUST
BYPASS TRUST
SURVIVOR'S TRUST FOR WIFE 3
DERRICK
3 OTHER CHILDREN
WIFE 3'S FAMILY
CORNWALL COPYRIGHT 2006 --ANY QUESTIONS?

CHAPTER TWENTY

Before You Make An Appointment

You have now made it through the middle of the estate planning game, rounded third and are heading for home to whatever expert, whether it is an attorney, a CPA, or an investment advisor, you have chosen to help you understand the tax tool application of the concepts you have just learned. You should have your own flow chart in hand, and perhaps written questions you need answered personally so you can customize an estate plan that best meets your vision and individual family dynamics.

How much of the book did you actually read, and how long did it take you? For some, it took a day. For others it took six months to get half way through before they decided to have someone else design an estate plan for them. And that is okay too, because now you can speak the language, or at least part of it, and that will give you more value for the time you will be paying your experts in the field.

There are alternative routes you can take before going straight to an attorney. These companies are called "wealth management advisors." These companies usually include a team (in this case the "team" is made up of a "network" of experts who are independent contractors located in their own offices) and may include an investment advisor, a CPA, an insurance broker, a transfer tax specialist, and an attorney who will all scrutinize your estate plan to ensure it achieves your vision. It is what has been called a "consultative wealth management process." Many banks also offer this service.

It is their job to make certain your needs are properly communicated, examined, and then put into a structure that would realistically meet your goals. It is a great concept to think you have all these experts working for you, but as with all businesses, it will work only as good as the people who run it. If they have the virtues of George Washington, who as a child when asked if he chopped down the cherry tree, responded, "I cannot tell a lie, I did it!" then you are in good hands.

But nobody knows you and your family better than you do. In this case, we are talking about those who have accumulated far more wealth then they had even hoped for, and now need all the help they can get. Can you imagine trying to invest an estate plan of $10 million when the marital tax exemption is only one million and the government takes 55% of the rest? Well, then try $1.5 million.

The first distinction to understand is the difference between **estate planning** and **financial planning.**

Estate planning uses trusts and wills to build a legal machine (on paper) that controls how you can distribute and protect your assets during your life, and to provide a secured legacy for your family after death.

Financial Planning helps you attain your financial goals while you are supporting your desired lifestyle and funding your retirement. A good financial plan builds your legacy.

It is important to understand this difference, because financial planners and advisors are selling a product, while an estate planner is selling his services. The purpose of this book, or the duty of an attorney, for example, is to help identify your goals, help determine your needs, and help formulate a plan to meet those goals and needs. It is not to profit from them.

Estate planning and financial planning are two components to consider when evaluating your overall financial picture. You want those experts to be in agreement to have the best chance of reaching your "wealth management" goals.

The goal for any trustee is to preserve capital and distribute it according to your wishes. You can always go back and adjust your Revocable Trust or rewrite your Will while you are alive, but after you are gone, your estate plan must be strong enough to reach into the future, but flexible enough to change with the times, i.e. family problems or a changing tax code.

Estate planning, in the broadest sense, is the accumulation, conservation, and distribution of wealth in a manner that most efficiently and effectively accomplishes your goals. Obviously it is a goal-oriented activity that uses tax minimization tools to distribute most of your wealth to your children, charities, education, special needs, etc.

After reading this book and strategizing with your attorney, you should be able to achieve these goals.

On the other hand, you are not going to die tomorrow (hopefully) and must make financial decisions based on your risk tolerance, as well as long term security options as you prepare for the unforeseen. But once you bring insurance into any financial or estate plan, it intrinsically brings a salesperson to the table who makes his or her living selling insurance. Nevertheless, insurance is a product every plan should consider from a wide range of policies including accidental death insurance, supplemental disability and long term care insurance and its tax ramifications.

Long Term Health Care

Long term care insurance is an important topic and really not as complicated as it appears to be. Long term care insurance is medical insurance that begins for you or your parents approximately 90 days after becoming so ill or incapacitated that you will need to move into a skilled nursing facility, or have a live-in nurse at your home. It means you will probably need skilled nurses to tend for you until you die.

What would you do if your loved one was faced with long term care needs and you were not properly insured? Today's prices for skilled-nursing homes are between four and seven thousand dollars per month. For example, taking the mid-range nursing care ($5,500) for pricing purposes means it would cost $66,660 per year to provide for the care for you, your spouse or your parent. *Unfortunately, Medi-care or Medicaid does not pick up a penny of this cost after the first 100 days.*

The average stay in such a facility is three to four years, but there are no guarantees your stay will not exceed seven years. Therefore, it is not difficult to calculate the total out of pocket costs. The catch is that to buy a long term care policy, the annual cost is determined by your age and your health record. If you have already had a heart attack or have a pacemaker, many companies would automatically disqualify you.

You just are not able to get insured, regardless of the price of the annual premium.

I am 58 years old, and recently received three quotes for $3,689.00, $3,439.37, and $4,138.89 per year, for the duration of my life or until I was placed in a skilled nursing facility, or had skilled nursing at my home. Going back to statistics, long term care insurance is usually not needed until you are in your eighties. Since there is nothing in the policy that guarantees these annual rates will stay the same, or the benefits of the policy will not change, I could statistically pay for 22 years while waiting to become sick enough to require skilled nursing care.

Twenty-two years at $3,689 annually amounts to $81,158. That is how much I would pay for a long term care plan that would pay for six years of my stay at a skilled nursing facility. Assuming it began when I turned 80 tears-old. The policy comes with a maximum payout benefit of $438,000 even if I lived to be 90 (by that time I would have paid $36,890 more). It has a compound inflation protection at 5% of the daily benefit of $200 beginning at age 58. Is that a good deal? Probably only if you need it and do not have it. Compare it to investing $3,600 a year with a 6% return for 22 years; therein lies the rub.

The annual premium is tax deductible, so that is good. Not having the insurance when you need it could clean out your bank account, which is bad. Given my family's lack of longevity, my risk tolerance encourages me not to pay the potential $81,158, or more. This takes into account that I own at least one extra asset that could be sold in the event I needed the care. So you must also take into account whether you have any large assets, besides your home, which could be sold, should the day come you need specialized care and this asset could pay for it. The fact is, around 85% of people need long term care at some point in their life, and that is a lot of people.

The biggest consideration for anyone thinking about long term care insurance is when you should start purchasing the policy. The annual premiums mentioned above become considerably higher, and your physical exam and health records more closely scrutinized to determine whether you are eligible for their insurance program, as you get older.

For the benefit of a 74-year-old client of average afflictions, I obtained three quotes for his age group. The premiums came back from the three largest insurance companies, just as the ones above, at the rates of $10,825.20, $8,362.22, and $10,127.06 each year. Needless to say the benefits work differently, and you will need an expert to explain it to you if you are interested in obtaining the insurance at age 74.

However, if the 74-year-old man paid one $10,825.20 premium, and six months later needed a skilled home care facility, then after 90 days of paying out of his pocket for his skilled care, his insurance benefits would begin and he would pay no more premiums. Of course, this is why insurance companies have medical exams and scrutinize medical records, both before and after, they have received your premium payment.

This is a risky bet for the 74-year-old because he may live to be 90, and will by then have paid $173,203 for $394,200 in lifetime benefits that are only good for three years. The point is that age makes a substantial difference as far as your premium, when it begins, and how long it lasts.

These are all risks you have to measure against the facts. If you sell a rental house to cover the cost of skilled care, instead of having insurance, you have lost an income producing resource. And, if you ever miss a single premium payment for your long term policy, you will lose your right to the policy by default. That is a harsh penalty and requires an automatic payment from your bank account to eliminate any default possibility. Unfortunately, if the bank makes the mistake, you will have to sue them to correct it. It is as though none of these institutions are really there to help you, only to take what is yours if there is a possibility you cannot outlast them -- so be careful!

Planning For Medicaid

Assume your father, whom you love dearly, is beginning to "wander" and becomes increasingly unable to manage his affairs because of Alzheimer's. He is going to need long term health care in a skilled nursing facility, or perhaps even a "secure parameter facility." That is one of every family's worse nightmares. The average time spent in such a facility is three years. The average expenses are $4,000 to $7,000 per month.

When preparing for such a calamity, it is widely assumed that a person with substantial assets is not eligible for the federally funded health insurance program, known as "Medicaid" throughout the United States, but "Medi-Cal" in California. Owning assets does not disqualify a person from Medi-Cal or Medicaid.

The money for an elderly, needy person that comes from Medicaid or Medi-Cal is a "loan" from the state, and needs to be paid back from the beneficiary's personal estate after the surviving spouse dies. The goals for an attorney in Medi-Cal and Medicaid planning are threefold:

First, use Medi-Cal as a means to get an immediate reduction in the cost for a skilled nursing facility. If the cost is $7,000 a month, the Medi-Cal benefits may be approximately $3,000 per month, saving the patient $3,000, by only having to pay $4,000 per month out of pocket. The situation regarding the payback from the estate may be different in your state which is why you need the assistance of a professional.

Secondly, the goal is to reduce the patient's cost for skilled nursing care to $0.00 if possible.

Third, the goal is to protect the Medicaid patient's spouse from creditor claims, and to get the amount of money to be paid back to the state as low as possible. This is done on a case by case basis.

Are There Moral Issues?

There may be some moral issues regarding a beneficiary's responsibility to pay the money back to the state; or the fact an applicant may have transferred property out of their estate in the first place to become eligible for Medi-Cal. But California has a liberal policy regarding these issues and it can only be expected that a client will use the laws available to them.

For example, the state determines eligibility of an applicant by examining the value of their assets. In order to become eligible for Medi-Cal the applicant can only have "countable assets" that fall below the **$2,000** limit.

How would that be possible you might ask?

Certain assets are not counted for eligibility purposes if they are determined to be either "exempt" or "unavailable." Some of these assets may come as a surprise. Exempt or unavailable assets for eligibility may include:

- An income producing apartment house;
- Any residence where the applicant claims they have "intent to return home;"
- Both husband's and wife's IRA;
- A building owned with a partner who is unwilling to liquidate is considered "unavailable;"
- A building is "exempt" if it is assessed for tax purposes at a rate lower than the encumbrance on the building, e.g. a building purchased thirty years ago for $50,000 which now has a $500,000 refinance on it;
- Property in litigation is unavailable; and
- Annuities which are irrevocable and immediate are not available during the "string of income."

Property that is not exempt or unavailable must be transferred to somebody else in order not to be counted. That can be a very bad idea. Once money or property is transferred, it is done so irrevocably. These are the types of decisions that must be made two or three years in advance. The "improvident child" to whom it might be transferred has the right to waste it, sell it, give it away, or just never give it back.

It should be remembered that Medi-Cal and Medicaid are "public assistance" programs. It was not created to assist the rich, nor was it created to assist only the poor. But the world does not rotate around becoming eligible for it. In many cases transferring assets can create far more tax problems for the transferees than the money paid from the estate for the health care.

Medi-Cal and Medicaid cannot recover their benefits until after both spouses die.

CHAPTER TWENTY-ONE

Who Does Elder Law Affect?

Can you imagine a specialization in Elder Law in the days of George Washington? Specialization was not necessary because the general population's life expectancy was about 40 years-old for men and women. The population was mostly made up of sturdy middle class folks who shared feelings and expectations that could only best be expressed by the manifest destiny to "go west young man." During those times, every middle class citizen had equal of opportunities to make something of their life, and seldom did male and female children do anything less than improve on the job begun by their mothers and fathers. They did not have much time on earth to improve their lot in life, so entire families worked together to make life better.

With all the advances in medicine over the last 100 years, our elder population continues to grow. And, not only are there more people in our elder population, they are living longer. It is not unusual to see people in their 70's, 80's, and even 90's today, with the occasional 100th birthday celebration.

Elder law affects all the people who are closest to us – all of the most precious people in our lives. This means your mother and father, grandpa and grandma, and everyone else in the family circle, including neighbors and close friends. And yes, it will some day include you.

All of these people deserve respect and are entitled to be treated with dignity. For that reason the practice of elder law has a much more personal side to it than any other field of legal expertise.

Clients are normally introduced to elder law when one of their older family members become ill, become unable to care for themselves, or begin to lose the "capacity" to think for themselves. They have their good days and bad days, but gradually the symptoms of illness or dementia are creeping into their lives.

Dementia does not legally mean "incapacitated." The term "good days and bad days" should not be underestimated. In many cases the elderly may not be suffering from dementia at all. They may only seem temporarily incompetent due to symptoms of their medication, or depression, anxiety, or other mental disorders; or perhaps some visceral disease, diabetes, cancer or infection.

The list goes on, but it is important to consider these possible causes before you jump to the conclusion your father needs to execute a power of attorney naming you as his "agent" to handle all business and personal affairs. Before any such steps are taken your father should, quite literally, have his head examined, and his body too. This is normally done by two physicians to decrease the chances of bias. If he is not competent to sign a power of attorney, you will have to seek a conservatorship. That is really going to make you wish he had executed a Revocable Trust to handle this problem. This trust would add a seamless asset management transition (trustee to successor trustee) versus obtaining a conservatorship.

Undue Influence of a Caregiver

There is an entire history of undue influence and abuse of the elderly, which is the basis of the "Elder Abuse Laws." All of it surrounds the issue of an older person's "competency" and another person's undue influence on the incompetent. Listed below are many of the acts used as tell-tale signs of undue influence by a caregiver:

- Withholding mail;
- Withholding telephone messages;
- Limiting visitation by friends and family;
- Discussing transactions at inappropriate times and places;
- Obtaining access to bank accounts;
- Being named on a Power of Attorney;

- Using victim's property;
- Becomes the victim's only source of friendship; and
- Demands business be terminated quickly.

Needless to say, whenever a caregiver ends up with property that would otherwise have gone to the victim's family, the caregiver is going to be suspected of "abuse."

However, if the family waits until the elder dies before they take action, they may be prevented, or at least dissuaded, from bringing a lawsuit because it would violate the "no contest clause" in the elder's Will. (There are ways around this but it is costly.)

It is interesting to note the profile of the "typical" abuser. Lawyers are on notice to beware of that 42 year old single son or daughter who is living at home and taking care of their surviving parent. They could be the child for whom things never quite worked out. Their siblings are busy living their own lives, and there is no one the parent feels they can trust more than their own child.

The Elder's Capacity to Sign

The biggest issue in any elder law case is going to be whether or not the Mom or Dad, aunt, uncle, grandma, grandpa or the neighbor next door had the "competency" or "capacity" (the terms are used interchangeably) to sign the documents distributing power or property at the "time" they signed the documents.

There are three levels of capacity:

1. Testamentary capacity;
2. Contractual capacity; and
3. Donor Capacity.

If any of the aforementioned documents are contested by an heir or beneficiary under the trust, it is these three levels of capacity that will be questioned by the court to determine if the signatory had the legal capacity to sign. Of the three capacities, "testamentary" requires the least amount of competency and "donor" requires the most.

"Testamentary power" is necessary for a person to sign a valid Will. It means they are able to, a.) verify they know what property they own, i.e., the extent of their "bounty," and b.) understand the natural objects of their bounty, i.e., can identify their family members who would normally inherit their property.

"Contractual capacity" is necessary to sign a Durable Power of Attorney or Health Care Directive. This capacity requires the person be able to communicate, understand, and appreciate the decision at issue and the significant benefits, risk, and alternatives of that decision.

"Donor capacity" is that capacity required when the signatory starts putting his/her estate into an irrevocable trust or gives it away to the caregiver. You really need to know what you are doing to sign a valid irrevocable trust!

To prove the applicable "capacity," evidence must be presented by way of opinions from doctors, lawyers, friends, and family, as well as tangible evidence tending to prove the state of the elderly (or debilitated) person's mind.

CHAPTER TWENTY-TWO

How much Does An Estate Plan Cost?

Value Based Pricing

The type of pricing you should be looking for in a law firm, or any firm for that matter, is one based on "unparalleled product satisfaction and consumer service." Pricing should always be under the client's control.

This recommended type of law firm operates on an innovative system called "value based pricing." The customer only pays for what he wants by knowing well in advance the price he is willing to pay. That also means they have to know what they want so an attorney can tell them how much it will cost. No consumer wants to contract for professional services when they do not know more than the hourly rate.

But that is exactly what most law firms expect of a potential client. The typical billing system is where the client agrees to pay the attorney for the hours they spend performing a particular job, and then wait in great trepidation to see the charge on their billing statement. This is only natural at $275 or more per hour.

How can a person feel they got their money's worth if they do not know the price they are going to pay? Satisfaction would be hard to guarantee. In addition, the price has to be equal to the value received for the client to feel good. Nobody wants to pay a Corvette price for a Mustang, yet they both drive you where you want to go.

In estate planning with a value based firm, you are able to build your own vehicle. If you want high performance down to the last QTIP, there is a price for that. If you want it straight and to the point, there is a price for that too.

The fact of the matter is everyone's needs are different. But regardless of needs, you must be assured the attorneys using value based pricing are based on the most "efficacious" services.

"Efficacious" in this context means a price based on the lawyer's "ability to accomplish a job with the minimum expenditure of time and effort." This is what is known as "value" in the world of legal services.

It is not based on the size of your estate or the overhead of the attorney. The fee is based solely on what you are willing to pay, or you should try to find another attorney. If you cannot find one at your price, then you are probably being unreasonable.

If you later decide you want the attorney to work beyond the scope of your work order, you may place a "change order." This way the client is always in control of the price by contracting for exactly what they want in a service contract, or in this case, an attorney/client fee agreement. It is a statement of fact, however, that implementing your plan with an attorney is a creative process. People are constantly changing their minds. Each time they do, it cost them more money. That is your best reason for being prepared and deciding what you want before you see an attorney.

Each client's estate plan should be an individual legal tapestry woven for your needs as determined from your answers to the interview questions. Some are simple and others are elaborate and take a great deal of time to complete. More often then not, the client will change their mind in the middle of the process. That does not undo the work that was already completed, but the value has been changed by the client who asks for more than he contracted for, even though the document may have the same name. It is still going to raise the cost of preparing the documents - so be prepared.

You want to go into the relationship assured of what you want, but open to suggestions if a better way exists.

All combinations of estate planning are unique because of the professional service that accompanies them. Here are some typical documents you should expect for your money:

Single person:

One Revocable Trust
One "Pour-Over" Will
One Advance Health Care Directive
One Durable Power of Attorney for Property Management
One Trust Transfer Deed
Notary Services
Unlimited assistance

One married couple:

One Joint Revocable Trust
"Pour-Over" Wills
Two Advance Health Care Directives
Two Durable Powers of Attorney for Property Management
Certification of Trust
One Trust Transfer Deeds
Notary Services
Unlimited assistance

Married couple w/children:

One Joint Revocable Trust
Two "Pour-Over" Wills
One Guardianship Directive
Two Advance Health Care Directives
Two Durable Powers of Attorney for Property Management

Marital Property Agreement
Tangible Personal Property
Memorandum
Certification of Trust
Two Trust Transfer Deeds
Trust Funding Assistance
Notary Services
Unlimited Assistance

A married couple w/children, children from a previous marriage, and other beneficiaries:

One Joint Revocable Trust, including:
One Survivor Trust
One Bypass Trust
One QTIP Trust (if needed)
Two "Pour-Over" Wills
One Guardianship Directive
Two Advance Health Care Directives
Two Durable Powers of Attorney
Marital Property Agreement
Tangible Personal Property memo
Certification of Trust
Trust Transfer Deeds
Trust Funding Assistance
Notary Services
Unlimited Assistance

There are many reasons why none of the above combinations are right for you. It depends on your personal, family and financial needs.

Why Your Estate Plan Must Be Reviewed

As the Greek philosopher Heraclites claimed as an axiom of eternal truth, "The only thing that remains the same is constant change." Because the times are still changing so should your estate plan when certain events arise.

Your plan needs to be reviewed and updated on a periodic basis, such as every three or four years as the children advance from high school to college to marriage, to divorce, or whenever you have a "life event."

It is malpractice for an attorney not to advise his client in writing that they should update and revise their will after their divorce has been finalized, or even before. Other routine changes that trigger an automatic review of your Revocable Trust or Will are marriages and/or separation after marriage, a new birth or death in the family, a change in your job or financial fortune, inheritance from your parents, a change in your health condition, and changes in taxes, to name a few.

Consider one of the most routine facts of life that strike 50% of American families. Assume your son or daughter, whom you love dearly, has chosen to marry the wrong individual. It may seem obvious to you that your child's divorce is imminent if they do not change their ways, but it may take years for them to figure that out.

Assume your Will or Trust leaves the full value of your estate to your child at age 30 and they are now turning 28. It seemed like a good idea ten years ago to leave money to them at such a mature age, but now you know the money would only be squandered on nothing productive. This is when you need to review your trust or Will and change the final distribution date to your child to the age of, say, 40.

Some people do not even realize this power is available to them. They think once the decision has been made and the documents are signed, it has been cast in iron. This is not so. Another common example of a reason for a change is news of a terminal illness for the spouse who was expected to outlive their partner. This happens often enough, and changes have to be made at the time to save on taxes.

Lastly, given the fact the entire federal estate tax plan is going to be repealed in the year 2010, your estate plan may have to be modified, and definitely should be reviewed. But it is not a good reason for those of you who prefer to procrastinate to wait until after 2010 to create your estate plan.

Finding the Attorney

Many people erroneously believe that to get the best representation you must pay the highest dollar to the largest law firm. Nothing could be further from the truth. Size has nothing to do with quality. The right hand in many large firms does not know what the left hand is doing. You pay for their expensive taste and lavish overhead by being charged $2.50 a page for a single photocopy.

In this day of modern technology, any solo practicing attorney sitting at their desk has the advantage of having a thousand law clerks at their beck and call. What was once the province of the large and prestigious law firm is now at the fingertips of any attorney who subscribes to Lexis or Westlaw, the two largest legal resources in the United States. There is no limitation on an attorney's ability to get answers fast from these internet resources.

Therefore, you can hire any attorney with confidence and not feel guilty that you are settling for something less just because he or she has a solo practice with one paralegal and maybe one secretary.

Many times throughout this book it has been recommended you seek the advice of a tax expert. In fact, it bears repeating that you will need to seek expert advice from a certified estate planning specialist, tax attorney or CPA anytime you are attempting to use complex trusts or business entities to transfer wealth, avoid tax consequences, or governmental regulations.

This is particularly true in areas that involve planning for Medi-Cal, Medicaid, Special Needs Trusts, Family Limited Partnerships or LLCs, and tax issues for domestic partnerships to name just a few more.

The certified experts are expensive, but they are worth it. In the long run, if they could not save people like you thousands of dollars, they would not have a job. There are many, many ways to save money on taxes and savings that are simply beyond the scope of this book. This book stops with the basic information you need to know, but there is so much more to learn.

Scams: A Friendly Warning to the Wise

Beware of estate planning tax scams and the con men (or women) selling them. Do not believe a word if something appears too good to be true. There is no cutting edge "pure" trust or "unincorporated organization" that allows you to not pay any taxes. Nor is there some new tax plan so clever that attorneys have not yet heard of it. "No, Virginia, there is no Santa Claus."

The only thing more outrageous than these promises of estate planning promotions are their appeal to hard working Americans. The con men tell you these are the same closely guarded trusts used by the Rockefellers and the Kennedy Foundation to keep their fortunes intact for generations. They claim that not only can you pay yourself in dividends which are "never subject to taxes," but your assets held in a PURE TRUST are "beyond the reach of probate and inheritance tax laws."

Do not believe it. There is no such thing. These scams, and what is known as a "living trust mill" where Living Trusts are churned out through seminars using pre-printed forms and no availability to a lawyer, are fairly common. The illegal ones are sometimes shut down by your local district attorney's office, and in many cases the scammers are prosecuted and the victims must answer to the IRS.

But these professional cons come back months or years later using different colors, names, faces, brochures, and definitely different catch phrases. "Pure" trust will be changed to "constitutional" trust, and instead of using the Rockefellers, they will be friends of the "Alliance for Mature Americans."

For your information, the statute of limitations for the IRS is three years from the date filed or from the date due. That three years works both ways: if you made a mistake on your taxes you have three years to amend those tax forms, after which you live with your mistake. But there is no statute of limitations for fraud.

CHAPTER TWENTY-THREE

When Death and Divorce Cause a Transmutational Wreck

Back in the days of George Washington, who died on the Saturday night of December 14, 1799, there was not the need for divorce that plagues our country today. The mortality rate was so high, and with a life expectancy of forty, it was rare a couple remained together for very long because usually one of them would die young.

Think of Martha Washington. She bore four children to her first husband and two of them died before reaching the age of six. Then her husband died and at age 26 she married George. She buried her last two children well before she died herself. With such a significant mortality rate in every family it caused neighboring families to join together in order to survive. For George Washington himself, the fact Martha was much richer than she was homely, probably prevailed over today's concept of "true love." But as for faithful and loyal to his wife, there was no man more true.

Now jump into the mores of virtuous conduct of today's society where, if you took your attorney's advice, you would begin preparing for a divorce before you ever got married, beginning with a prenuptial agreement with your wife or husband to be. Being an attorney myself, I cannot dissuade a couple from going through the prenuptial process, if for no other reason than it will help you define what belongs to each spouse from the very start. Such a document would make the likelihood of an open and honest conversation about estate planning much easier by reminding each spouse how they came into the marriage, and how they intended to hold title to their property in the event of a divorce, or death. Hopefully the prenuptial was done correctly, with two attorneys, so as to avoid accusations of taking advantage.

On the other hand, the mere mention of a prenuptial agreement is enough to send some romantics over the edge. Regardless of how they may have felt at the time they signed the prenuptial agreement, it was prepared before they began living in the separate properties to which they have no right, but have come to consider as their own. This may be due to referring to the property as "our" house, and remembering all the ideas they had for remodeling the interior design.

With that said, what could be more depressing than a discussion about death and divorce? What is more heartbreaking? But for some, this trauma is exacerbated by in-fighting over property rights between parents, and/or between children, but particularly between "blended family" members. The issue is the same whether the dispute arises out of death or divorce. The answer to who is entitled to reimbursement for money invested in specific family properties is found in the legal term, "transmutation of property."

"Transmutation" is the process by which the property rights of married persons are changed from separate property to community property, or vice versa. This transmutation may be done through written agreements between husband and wife for various reasons at any time in their marriage. This includes, but is not limited to, the great tax advantage upon the death of the first spouse, as explained in Chapter Four, that comes from switching from joint tenancy to community property.

Characterization of property at death is crucial because it identifies how much of the estate each spouse is allowed to pass on to his or her heirs. This is called the "power of appointment." Husband and wife are each entitled to will, devise or bequest their 50% share of the community property to whomever they please. But they have 100% power of appointment over their separate property.

This is where death and divorce can cause a transmutational wreck. **There is a big difference between the transmutation of property when you are getting divorced or when you are determining ownership rights after death.**

For divorce purposes, any separate property that was contributed to the marriage to purchase community property can be traced back, and the contributing party has a right to reimbursement upon divorce. (California Family Code § 2640)

But this is not the law upon death, and although it is the general rule in most states, this is why you need to use a local attorney to make certain that is so in your state. After death, transmutation becomes a permanent one-way transaction that is a non-recognized event. This means it cannot be undone, and the contributing party is not entitled to reimbursement.

It must be pointed out however, in a transmutation agreement where one spouse receives a more generous benefit from the other spouse, and it appears unfair to the giving spouse, there must be a letter of acceptance from the receiving spouse to complete the transaction. Otherwise, the agreement will be voidable in a court of law. The transmuted property will be returned to the estate of the giving spouse as separate property.

I point this out only because the law books are filled with cases where the attorney who drafted the transmutation agreement did not complete the transaction by drafting a letter of acceptance from the receiving spouse because...actually, I do not know why. Perhaps it escaped his mind after drafting the initial document, or maybe he had not read the law on this subject lately. The law is constantly changing.

This is why you want to use an attorney. If the surviving spouse has the transmutation agreement voided by a child of a previous marriage, she then has someone to hold liable for the damages. I am not trying to encourage malpractice lawsuits. I am trying to encourage you to let an attorney help you with your estate plan. This is what they do for a living and they can be very helpful.

Voidable agreements can create unnecessary surprises for heirs to an otherwise well planned estate. This book cannot resolve all the conflicts that may arise over the ownership of property. These conflicts must be examined on a case by case basis. They could only be avoided if people lived in the ideal attorney's world I have spoken of. This is a world where all potential liabilities are foreseen and all reasonable precautions are taken well in advance so as to not allow any damage to be done, and that is something that is just not possible.

But even in cases where the intentions of the parties are clear, it does not mean it will work out that way. As one astute legal scholar observed, **"There is something wrong in the law where justice enjoys the power of making odd results that hurt the expected person to benefit."**

No truer words have been spoken about the legal system.

This is in reference to cases where separate property rights are held to be community property, and children from a previous marriage are denied their inheritance; or, where a father's gift to a daughter is denied because she was a step-child from a prior marriage, even though he raised the child for twenty years. In order to avoid these types of injustices, the married couple must take every opportunity to make their intentions as clear as possible.

In an ideal attorney's world all couples, prior to marriage, would sit down and begin preparing for their divorce. They would each put their separate property in a "separate property trust." In this fashion it would be difficult for them to commingle their funds without intentionally doing so, and if they do not commingle, it is not community property, and would not need to be traced back in case of divorce.

A separate property trust would be a great property identifier and much cleaner than a "premarital contractual agreement" (aka "prenuptial agreement").

Who Polices Estate Planning?

The short answer to who polices these trust transactions is the IRS. Tax statements must be filed and the IRS has three years to uncover mistakes.

In reality, the integrity of the trust business is regulated by the attorneys and CPA's who are charged with the job. Much of an attorney's continuing education in estate planning deals with ethical duties and obligations to the client.

The relationship between client and attorney is extremely confidential. You must be able to confide in them and fully expect that they will protect what they have heard privately. This is the only way to develop the kind of relationship necessary to get the job done right.

CHAPTER TWENTY-FOUR

Domestic Partners and Possible Same Sex Marriage

On September 19, 2003 California passed into law Assembly Bill 205, commonly known as the California Domestic Partners Rights and Responsibilities Act of 2003. It was designed to accommodate the over 100,000 households in California headed by same sex partners. It also benefits older heterosexual couples, where one partner is over 62 years old and looking for an alternative to marriage.

However, the word "benefit" in this context must be used carefully. The Act provides exactly what the name implies, which is rights *and* responsibilities. But the responsibilities may be more than those persons living an unconventional lifestyle have bargained for, and the rights may be far less than they had hoped for.

Since the law only became effective on January 1, 2005, every case has to be analyzed individually. There is a dearth of case law to help attorneys advise their clients, and the tax ramifications must be submitted to tax experts in this new field of practice.

The purpose of the law is to confer same sex couples the same equality and status as the spousal rights conferred on married couples. But it doesn't turn out that way for many same sex couples.

Denial of Federal Benefits

On a federal level the state status of a "domestic partner" has been preempted by what is known as the Defense of Marriage Act Statutes, or DOMA. Also passed by 40 other states, the federal DOMA holds that the California Domestic Partnership Act has no bearing on the federal definition of "marriage" or "spouse," and will not qualify domestic partners for the Section 1138 federal benefits that accompany traditional marriages between a man and a woman.

In plain language this means that federal rights normally granted to a "spouse" are denied to domestic partners. This includes:

- Social Security benefits to a surviving spouse;
- Veteran's benefits such as disability, dependency or death benefits to spouses;
- Tax consequences: 179 provisions of tax law, including the unlimited marital deduction upon the first spouse's death!

- Employment protection: no entitlement to ERISA.

Depending on your status, these denials could work against you if, when deciding to be a stay-at-home partner, you thought you would be eligible for your partner's federal pension.

Welcome to the World of State Benefits

California's law is one of the most far-reaching in the country. Couples who qualify, by registering with the Secretary of State, are entitled to equal state-conferred rights regarding the following benefits. They all carry heavy responsibility:

- Financial support, including "spousal" (partner) support;
- Mutual responsibility for debts to third parties;
- Access to superior court for dissolution of relationship;
- Standing to assert legal claims based on marital status, employment rights for family care, medical and bereavement leave;
- Child custody and visitation, and child support;

- Communication privileges, including the right not to testify against your partner; and

Most importantly, for estate planning purposes, a domestic partner gets an identifiable status in probate court. You are no longer a "stranger at law" with no status. You take the place of the "spouse" in the scheme of intestate succession.

Previously, family members could attack this non status partnership as collusion for fraud, or make serious accusations regarding coercion and undue influence to receive an inheritance.

The domestic partner now has a right to oversee their deceased partner's remains, including anatomical gifts, consent to autopsy, and arranging burial in family cemeteries.

A Domestic Partnership is Not a Political Statement

There are so many uncertainties in this new law that it is difficult to advocate that someone should register without first examining their needs and expectations very closely.

Entering into a domestic partnership is definitely not something you do to make a political statement. Anybody who signed up to support the gay and lesbian rainbow coalition at the park rally years ago is in for a rude awakening.

You could register in the year 2000. In 2003 the law was passed, but it did not become effective until 2005. Then the law was made retroactive and everyone who had previously signed up was now legally bound to the partnership. All the rules and regulations regarding community property rights applied, and a divorce was necessary to dissolve the obligation.

As a practical matter this means some people didn't even know they were legally bound to each other, let alone that half of their earned income over the last five years belonged to their domestic partner.

Another concern is the fact that the jobless partner could now take the hard working partner to court and receive half the community estate, going back for perhaps as long as they were domiciled together.

Bottom Line for Domestic Partners

The law essentially defines domestic partners as single persons with community property. Therefore, one of the best ways for a partner to provide for the surviving partner is for each partner to keep their property separate and not commingled. Then upon the death of the first partner they can provide an irrevocable trust for the benefit of the surviving partner, such as a Bypass Trust, that will not be added back into the partner's estate upon their death. The benefits go to the surviving partner, and the remainder to whomever they agree.

A recent ruling by the California Supreme Court on May 15, 2008 allows same sex couples to wed. There is really nothing for gay and lesbian couples to celebrate over yet, other than the moral victory the court gave by ruling they could wed. The court stated that not allowing same sex couples to wed would be against the State of California's constitution. That appellate decision is presently on appeal before the United States Supreme Court, but if it follows in the shoes of its Massachusetts predecessor in 2004, the Supreme Court will refuse to hear the case, making it valid law. The Massachusetts' legislators refused to amend their state constitution disallowing same sex marriages

Presently, in California, the backlash of the court's opinion had garnered enough signatures among the citizens of California to allow the right to gay marriage to be put to a vote in the general election of November 2008. Until then it is interesting to note that at in least one county, Kern County, the court's administrator has decided the courts will no longer allow same sex marriages, stating the backlog of cases as its reason.

These state court rulings have no effect on the federal law restrictions against gay marriages. The right to a gay marriage carries no further rights than the Domestic Partnership and Responsibility Act of 2003. Gay marriage, at best, would be a formality for love, but with little meaning other than that because it gives no more rights to the wedded gay couple than those outlined above in the Act of 2003.

It is advisable to approach the same sex marriage with caution *because nobody knows* what the legal ramifications will be years from now. It could possibly make the dream of gay marriage into a red tape nightmare that further complicates your federal rights, particularly in the event of a divorce.

CHAPTER TWENTY-FIVE

Empowerment for Baby Boomers

The goal of this book is to give everyone who reads it the ability to know what they are talking about. You must have some idea of where you want to go, and what you want to do, when you begin estate planning. You are an intelligent person and this book will give you everything you need to know to protect your family and to make you a hero as long, as you are not afraid to ask for a little help.

Ask yourself, where have all the heroes gone? Can you possibly imagine what it must have taken for Washington to keep 10,000 troops together in the winter of 1877-1878? Sixty percent of the revolutionary army was either diseased, or were so ill equipped they could not be moved into action. These soldiers knew their families and children back on their farms were all freezing and starving to death, and yet, this one man, this leader of men, never left their side. He demanded more of these soldiers than could possibly be expected of them, eventually leading them to victory, after an eight year struggle, against the tyranny of King George III and his forces. We have no idea what sacrifices this required.

How did Washington do it? He would never stop fighting for freedom. Regardless of the many battles he lost he would never surrender, and he could always instill this spirit and extract another battle from his weary troops.

What kind of man could accomplish that feat against the best professional army in the world? Think for one moment the make-up and the character of the man who, after suffering nothing but defeats at the hands of the British soldiers early in the war, proceeded to lead this rag-tag revolutionary army across the ice strewn and snow driven Delaware River at night on Christmas Eve, 1776.

In defiance of all his advising generals who believed they would be slaughtered by such an outlandish plan, they nevertheless followed their general, catching the enemy by surprise and turning the tide of the war. This daring victory, heartened the troops, and caused them to forego their furlough and fight on for one more month, and then another.

Was he brave? Was he ingenious? Is there any doubt his integrity, honesty and his work ethic? He led by example, and that was what held those soldiers together. Many had no shoes or boots for the fiercest of winter river crossings. What a feat to get into those boats for a surprise attack on the fearsome Hessians -- regardless of what the outcome may have been. He never considered surrender, not ever. He just kept on fighting until he wore the British out.

George Washington was the same hero who then led this new country as a citizen serving as its first president. He set the bar for all those who were to follow. He was the first President to ever emancipate his slaves, doing so upon his wife's death. In terms of leadership ability in the culture of that time, what more could you ask of a United States citizen in 1799?

This is how you get your estate plan done:

1. converse honestly;
2. list your property;
3. decide on your beneficiaries;
4. decide which trusts to use;
5. make sure you understand;
6. envision the big picture;
7. write out your vision;
8. seek help from experts;
9. make certain it's done your way;
10. relax and enjoy your heroism.

Let me assure you, if you own two or more houses, or you own one house worth over a million dollars, and you have children from a previous marriage, and you have remarried and now have children from your new, or newer, marriage, then your task of providing an estate plan is like nothing you have ever done before.

And, if it is your desire to leave this earth on your own terms, with the legacy you worked for intact, and 55% of it not taken by the government, then plan on buckling down and following the procedures in this book. No one is telling you it is easy. You have to be prepared to think.

Now is the time to accept the challenge of creating your estate plan, but that is actually only half the job. If it is done right, and that means in accordance with the IRS Code and Regulations, it will have taken enough thought and research that when you die you will be leaving behind a 35 page joint Revocable Trust. Then the second job starts. It requires funding the sub-trusts, filing tax returns, notifying beneficiaries, obtaining valuations, making decisions between exempt and non-exempt marital trust and the formula upon which they are funded. The surviving trustee will probably need the assistance of an attorney to help administer the trust at the start, just to make sure it is done right.

Or, you can do it the easy way by doing nothing, and then praying there will be no selfish heir who thinks they know better than you, and is waiting for the opportunity to show the entire family. That would be an example of a person who failed to leave a hero's legacy.

CHAPTER TWENTY-SIX

Step by Step Planning

What follows is a fictionalized train of thought that goes into any baby boomer's attempt to plan their estate. If he, let's call him Mark Cornwall (that sounds like a nice name), wanted to sit down and write out what he has learned from this book, and apply it to a plan to distribute his and his wife's own legacy, it would go something like this:

As explained in Chapter Eleven, every state's rules of intestate succession are extremely favorable to the surviving spouse. Since my spouse has no blood lineage to my daughter from a previous marriage, my daughter, Maxine, (thirty years old), could wind up with very little, if any, of my personal property, depending upon my wife's generosity and kindness. There is no doubt in my mind about the generosity and kindness of my wife toward my daughter, but that is not the purpose of an estate plan. The purpose is to put presumptions aside and state exactly how I want things to be done. I have been remarried for six years, but I have had my daughter for thirty years. My wife and I lost a son. Perhaps things will change, but I must work with what I have now, or know I will have later.

The quote by Justice Brandeis is what I must live by in the context of estate planning. By taking a little more time, and working a little harder, I will be rewarded because I will not have to pay the same toll as those people who were too busy, or who did not care enough, to worry about it.

The attributes of a well planned estate came to me as an epiphany. I was always too busy, or too young, I thought, to do anything about it now.

Then I had my estate plan drawn up by an expert in the field. My wife, who holds a Jurisprudence Doctorate, and I spent the requisite two hours or so in his office explaining to him, how we wanted to distribute the estate should something happen to either of us. We then waited about a month to receive our rough draft. Quite typically, I set it on the corner of my desk and stared at it for another month because, of course, I was too busy to take care of that business. I sometimes thought, "What's the point, let them figure it out after I am dead." That is about as selfish as it gets.

But another reason behind this selfishness was that I knew nothing about how a good estate plan would actually work for me, my wife and my daughter. Nor did I know how much money it would save me, because I did not even know what the marital tax exemption was, or that one even existed.

Deep in my mind was the fact that I know attorneys do make mistakes, and I wondered how I would know if he did or did not make one for me? All I was sure of was it would be too late to fix it after I was gone.

Then the day came when I decided to read my Revocable Trust. My wife had already read and signed it. It was a simple task for her, because she trusted the attorney to do it right, and it appeared to her that he had done so. It did not appear so to me. The estate consisted of five properties, three of them income producing, an island in Alaska, three corporations with minor interests, securities, investment interests, IRAs, several bank accounts, cash, earned income and a multitude of personal property.

The problem is that all of this was brought into the marriage by me, and although we had a prenuptial agreement that extended out ten years, a term I thought long enough to determine if you really loved someone or not, we had only been married for two years when we drafted the estate plan. As time moved on and I loved my wife more and more each day, a phenomenon I was not aware of happened. I began to feel that the prenuptial agreement was explicitly legal, but not particularly compassionate, considering what she did to improve my life. I was concerned this Revocable Trust would make me feel the same way as time went on. Of course, that is why it is "revocable," and looking back, it would have been much better than nothing.

But as I read the verbiage of the Revocable Trust I found it was couched in a language and a system I did not understand. I understood the gist of it, but it was thirty-five pages of ifs, ors and buts. In short, I would not have signed that document in a million years.

And that is when it came to me that as a 58-year-old baby boomer, I had never been taught the slightest thing about death and the inheritance system? I found there was nothing out there that explained the system and its lexicon in layman's terms. So I studied the book, ESTATE PLANNING: The Heroes Way for Baby Boomers, paid attention to the flowcharts and various scenarios of other baby boomer's visions of their legacy, and now I am ready to do my own.

I realized I had reached the second step after learning the subject matter. I needed to write my own estate plan to explain my desires, and do so like George Washington, because I am determined to get the job done.

Write Down What You Own

The key to writing your estate plan is realizing the process is an emotional experience. That is why you begin with the very ordinary and monotonous task of writing down all the property you own, or at least care to mention, and its value in dollars to you based on reasonable comparisons. We all know some things are priceless, but *really,* how much is it worth? You need to do this valuation to determine your eligibility for the marital tax exemption, and everything referred to in your Revocable Trust will in many cases only apply to community, separate or quasi-community property.

The exemption will revert back to $1 million in 2011, according to how the law is written at present. When that happens, it will include millions of more Baby Boomers who thought they were not going to have to pay a 55% tax because their estate was too small.

(This includes all the "older" people who have had enough time to accumulate well over that amount of assets. It was interesting to read one person's perspective that there should be no tax exemption on inheritance, because all babies should be born equal. Apparently this person had no hope for inheritance. That would be a person of extreme naïveté toward trust in the government's use of inheritance tax, and should be responded to by anyone who had their inheritance stolen from them.)

It will be appreciated by your beneficiaries if you add your comments regarding the gifts you list in your "schedule of properties." This will be your only chance to comment, unless you prefer doing it in the trust itself. This "schedule of properties" must be funded into the Revocable Trust in order to make it legal, and to keep you from having to go back to probate court. However, this is not the schedule of properties you want to attach to your Revocable Trust. On that one, you just want to list the properties.

On personal property you can use a bill of sale to transfer the property into the estate. Many people, including lawyers, do not even do that. But if people cannot agree on who gets what, it will wind up in probate court, if the intended gifts are not well defined.

There is a portion of your Revocable Trust that can be as informal as you would like, as long as your desires are clearly set out in plain language as to what the gift is and to whom it is going. This means to specify the beneficiary and the gift you are giving them. This part of the Revocable Trust falls under the division named "specific gifts." What follows is the way our fictional baby boomer, Mark Cornwall, decided to write out what his gifts are and how he and his wife, Renee, plan on giving them away. His plan was to just start writing in order to give it that personal touch. Nobody is encouraging you to copy his style. You are encouraged to write in your own style, much shorter, or much longer, whatever it takes to get it on paper:

"There is a life size wooden carving I purchased in La Paz, Bolivia, the highest capital city in the world, in 1977 when I was 27 years old. It is a wooden carving of an Inca warrior

replicating the messengers who carried everything from gold to fresh fish by running up the Andes to the ancient Inca capital of Machu Picchu, delivering it to the Chieftains. These messengers, starting from the coastal port of Lima, Peru, ran miles before starting the trail up the 3,000 meter mountain ridge, completing the trip in a single day.

The messenger was carved from a huge slab of mahogany, his body chiseled and adorned in his native dress, with an embroidered pack slung across his shoulder carrying...what? He is blowing a goat's horn to announce his arrival. Beautifully crafted, his calves and forearms are as muscular as you would imagine for a man to succeed on such a journey. Every detail is attended to in etching and various colors creating a warrior far beyond the western tobacco-shop Indian. I have never seen anything like it, and it has been 31 years.

After bargaining for several hours I purchased the carving for $200. I remember my pride walking down the cobblestone streets of La Paz, all the citizens looking at the grandeur of the carving I carried at shoulder height. I carried it to the Exprinter office, an international shipping company, to have a crate made to send it home. Exprinter wanted $275 to build the crate, as they obviously viewed me as a fool.

So I took the warrior over to Lufthansa Airlines and had it shipped to Los Angeles covered in heavy card-board. I put a hundred "FRAGILE" stickers on it before it was sent, and, miraculously, it arrived without a scratch.

That purchase was made 31 years ago and still hangs on my wall at home. The question is, how much is it worth? When it arrived in America in 1977 I put its value at $25,000, as it was of unquestionable quality and uniqueness. It was the kind of art piece you could not get without going to the highest capital city in the world, and there was not another one exactly like it in the world. So, for all these reasons, I would not sell it for a million dollars today, if for no other reason than it connects me with my youth in the wayfaring past.

The carving is rivaled among my possessions only by a Tibetan rug I purchased in 1983 off the loom of a woman weaving it in Tibet. The Tibetans are recognized as the finest rug makers in the world, and this rug displays the symbols of Health, Wealth, Wisdom and Spirituality better than any way the Dali Llama could meditate over. This treasure also hangs in my house above the fireplace. What is that worth? It cost me $500 from the Tibetan refugee, and I could have sold it for $5,000 upon returning home. But after the Maoists attempted to complete their genocide of the Tibetan culture, there are few refugees left with the art of true Tibetan rug making. They are definitely not rugs *to be walked on. So what is it worth? Again, it is not for sale, so who does it go to?*

In this same genre of "priceless" (sentimentally), I have a full size 30" walrus tusk that has a scene of the Alaskan Wild scrimshawed across it from end to end and signed by the Eskimo artist Joe Blatchford. The scrimshaw includes bald eagles, brown bears, cubs up a tree, a winter cache, geese and forest and mountains.

It was given to me by my friend, Paul Johnson, President of the Alaskan Iron Workers Union at the time, and a lifetime Alaskan. It had been in his family for thirty years before he gave it to me in 1980 as a trade for a piece of an island I own. Paul is gone now, and I am at a loss determining who could really understand the nature of this one-of-a-kind art piece by this Native artist. It has a true value near $50,000. Perhaps a native art museum would be interested, and that would allow for a healthy tax deduction. But I believe Paul would roll over in his grave if I thought of it as a tax deduction.

Then there is the skin of the boa constrictor that attacked me in 1974, at the confluence of the Amazon and Rio Negro Rivers at Ponta Negra in Manaous, Brazil. It is worth nothing, except my life and the memory of it. There is no monetary value there, but I wonder who would want it.

Then there is my gun collection:

Walther P-38 (1976);
Kimber 45 semi-automatic, (2000);
Remington Wingmaster 12 gauge pump, "For law enforcement only", (1979);
etc.

Who would I leave these fine pieces of weaponry to, my daughter or my wife? This is where I may as well start entertaining the thought of leaving gifts to friends and extended family. I would consider John, my daughter's boyfriend, if they were married, but who knows, she may have a child some day who enjoys target shooting or hunting or gun collecting. I know my daughter has no interest in it."

(About this time, Mr. Cornwall begins to realize he is getting a bit long winded rummaging down his collective personal goods.)

Unlike George Washington, the only other things I have worth mentioning are golden. There is the Bulova watch with gold nuggets soldered to the wrist band that was made during the pipeline days when money flowed like oil. That watch is my oldest, and most worn, material possession. I have worn it continuously for 29 years. Not a week goes by I don't get a compliment on it such as, "That should be in a museum." It is hard to put a price tag on that.

By now you get the idea about adding personal property items to your list and comments regarding their meaning to you. You may or may not enjoy, or like the idea. The point is that there is no law against it, and the beneficiary may find it a loving gesture. However, he could go on the more he thinks of it:

The more common personal property such as my three cars, the desk I just finished working on for three weeks to refurbish, family photos from the turn of the nineteenth century, first edition books such as one signed by James Fenimore Cooper in Pathfinder in 1897; one signed by Colonel Leroy McAfee, the man of whom Thomas Dixon wrote in The Clansmen (1905) which was the story behind the first movie ever made entitled, "The Birth of a Nation"; and the classic Cannery Row (1945) signed by John Steinbeck, are all items to be given away personally. Their meaning in history could be lost in a boilerplate phrase like, ***"To Frank's class, share and share alike."***

These **boilerplate** phrases are how 99% of boilerplate Revocable Trusts are drawn, which is of no use in resolving complaints.

But let's face it. When we are dead, people are only going to keep what they like and the rest is going to be given or sold to someone you do not even know. That is the reality of most situations, so why make it tough on yourself? It's their gift! But don't forget your collections, whether it be:

- *Franklin Mint Coins, Rembrandt Collection;*
- *Match-covers from around the world;*
- *Salt and pepper shakers;*
- *Carved wooden heads;*
- *Pocket knives;*
- *Sailing ships;*
- *And paintings, carvings, guitars, a piano, and about twenty other things that someone would like.*

Glory be to George Washington for keeping track of every possession, and knowing who to give it to, because we have not even started on the property acquisitions and the when, and what fors of how much, and to whom they must go in light of today's financing, and to avoid taxes.

You Should be Feeling Good

You should be feeling pretty good by now. You have accomplished your first major goal, and that is getting started. By now, you must have reached a comfort level on this enterprise because you got to rummage back through everything you own and how you got it. The fun of it is that there is nothing bad. They are all gifts for someone, from your fishing pole to your sewing machine and cookbooks.

Now comes the larger, or perhaps more valuable, accomplishments in life; those things that make up the American Dream. Here is the way Mark Cornwall wrote them down:

"1. There is the island in Alaska, purchased in 1978, value $250,000;

2. The 50% ownership of the condo in Pismo Beach, earned as interest in developing a 15 home subdivision in 1990; worth $135,000 in 1990, present value $425,000 in 2008;

3. The fourplex apartments on the beach in Carpinteria I purchased in 1990 for $475,000, and developed into four deluxe apartments beginning in 2000, value $1,495,200.

4. The Green and Green craftsman home I built in Pasadena in 1994, value, $1.8 million in 2008.

5. The 50% interest in a rental home in Lompoc, value $850,000 in 2008;

6. These mortgages will have to be paid from one property or another as provided in my Revocable Trust in order for everyone (my wife and daughter), to become a winner. In other words, something must be sold.

When it comes to what tools Mark is going to use to avoid the death tax, it is the same formula that is right for at least 50% of baby boomers who have also accumulated more than one real estate asset. He is going to have to give it all away, because you still cannot take it with you. However, you can give it away and still use it while you are alive.

"My mother, father and sister predeceased me. I have a brother, nine years older than I am, who is impossible to get along with. Regardless of how I have tried to reunite our relationship, it was much more painful than not having a relationship. He requested I never contact him again. That was three years ago, after many, many years of unhappiness for each of us. So I respect his wishes and do not communicate with him. Nor will he be included in the distribution of my estate."

Beware, if the above described relationship is not fiction in your family. If you have the same situation, you must specifically mention in your trust and your Pourover Will that you are aware of his or her existence and you are specifically leaving him or her nothing, otherwise he has a right to contest it in probate court, and you can believe he/she would. This is not child's play when it comes to siblings fighting over their parents' benefits.

When you add up the gross value of the real property in the estate itself, it comes to $4,387,500. This excludes the personal property, cars, artwork etc. That puts the estate $3,387,500 above the marital tax exemption of $1 million after 2010, and that amount would be taxed at the new 55%. If Mark Cornwall did nothing to avoid the estate tax on this property, that $3,387,500 over the marital tax exemption would cost his daughter $1,693,750 in estate tax. This could happen if his wife died simultaneously in the same plane crash, and he had not provided an alternative to this situation in their Revocable Trust.

Simultaneous Death

In the event of a simultaneous death, such as a plane crash, the wife's separate property, and one-half of the community property from the date of their marriage would go to her parents, and then to her brother and sister (in California). They would have to share in the payment of the 45% tax on the entire value over $2 million, if it was in 2008, and Renee's separate property was more than $2 million.

However, assuming it was 2011 and each spouse gets a $1 million marital tax exemption, the heirs would pay taxes for anything over the $1 million exemption to Renee's estate. But as we have seen, Renee does not have that much separate property. Therefore, if Mark wanted their estate plan to work as planned after a simultaneous death, he must write a provision in the Revocable Trust that California Probate Code § 220, (or whatever the statute is in your state) does not rule the outcome of the death of both spouses. It must be agreed to by both spouses that Mark Cornwall was the first spouse to die. This will assure both parties that your estate plan will work the way you wanted and Maxine, the daughter, will not get stuck with $1,693,750 in estate taxes.

Whenever there is a simultaneous death **the big issue will be, "who died first, making which spouse the surviving spouse?** You can see the crucial difference it would make if Renee was the surviving spouse, or if Mark was the surviving spouse.

California, as in the majority of states, has adopted the "Uniform Simultaneous Death Act." This law basically states that if a beneficiary's right to succeed to an interest in property is conditional upon surviving another person, and it cannot be established by clear and convincing evidence that the beneficiary survived, "the beneficiary is deemed not to have survived the other person."

Breaking this law down, it means that Renee, Mark's wife, will inherit certain properties through the Revocable Trust if Mark dies first, and if Renee dies first then the opposite occurs. The old law said she or he had to survive by only a second, then that changed to 120 hours, and now it must be shown by clear and convincing evidence, not by the former law's "sufficient evidence," that Mark or Renee died first. Otherwise, the property of each spouse is to be distributed as though each person survived; even though they died simultaneously. It is a legal hypothecation.

The purpose of such a law is to keep one side of the family from feuding with the other side over who gets what property. By law in California, Renee began owning one-half of everything Mark earned or purchased if it could be traced back to his community earnings beginning on their wedding day. Therefore, she would own one-half of their community property beginning the date of their marriage, along with whatever portion of Mark's or Renee's separate property they wanted to bequest to each other, or transmute to each other by agreement.

This entire complication of "simultaneous death" can be avoided, and you do not have to worry that your brother-in-law is going to end up owning your separate property, as long as you spell out your wishes in your Revocable Trust. This is reiterated in the Pourover Will. But half of the community property will always be Renee's separate property to do with as she pleases.

If you are thinking that going to all this trouble is not worth it because paying estate taxes is just the price of living in America, then you have not learned the motive of this book. But it is you who has to do something about it to avoid the tax. No one can do it for you.

Write Down the Names of Potential Beneficiaries

Now that you have gone through all of your tangible personal and real property, write down all the names of the potential heirs you would like to give something to, and what that gift might be. It does not matter if you give the same gift twice, if you cannot make up your mind. But it would be better to either split it, or come to a final decision. Otherwise, you would have to come back and change it in your trust. The important thing is to start writing ideas down to get started. They may be just ideas but you can always change them. That is what Revocable Trusts are all about.

I realize for some people from big families it is quite a chore to write down every heir you plan on leaving something to, but if you are leaving a gift to be split between classes of persons then you can just name the class. You can list people in groups or "classes," such as "Ben Cartwright's children" or "Suzy Smith's nieces and nephews" or "uncle Mark's issue" or perhaps "nieces only." State the gift in plain and simple language. The mental process used by our fictional Mark Cornwall can be applied to any size family, blended or not.

As for formality, you could copy the following gifting format and place it in the Revocable Trust verbatim. It does not require legal precision to name your property and state who you want to gift it to. The only legal requirement is that the property and person can be understood, and the property must be funded (transferred into the name of the trust) before you die. I cannot emphasize that too much; otherwise the Revocable Trust goes to probate if anything not funded is over $100,000.

As far as Mark Cornwall's family is concerned there is:

Renee, his wife;

Maxine, his daughter;

Mary, his mother in law;

Rodger, his father in law;

Frank, Renee's brother, Frank's wife Gilda, their children, Kathy, and nephew Tim. These can all be referred to as the "Frank family."

Then there is Pearl, Renee's sister, and her three children, Sam, Clare, and the newest addition, Elizabeth, with Pearl's significant other, Abe. In this situation you would want to be more specific as to who is in the Pearl family given the previous marriage, with two prior children.

Then there is Mark's side of the family: Renee, Maxine and her significant other, John. Additionally, there is their dog "Kili," short for Kilimanjaro, a Border Terrier, and Maxine's dog "Brooklyn," a Chihuahua. That is the entire Cornwall family. Yes, a dog can be in a family if you so specify, but if you actually want something specific to be set aside for the pet you need a pet trust.

Then there is Mark and Renee's extended family. For Mark, some of his extended family includes friends he has known since first grade. Listed in no particular order, they are Bruce, Walt, Jim, John, and Steve. All of them have proven to be brothers, unlike Mark's real brother.

Decide Which Properties are Gifted to Specific Beneficiaries

Next, write down your specific gift requests. It can look as simple as something like this:

Specific gifts:

"To Renee:

1. *The Pasadena house goes to Renee. We have executed a transmutation agreement regarding the property within the revocable trust which Mark agrees to transmute and Renee agrees to accept*

50% of ownership interest. In this manner Renee shall have the benefit from the "step-up" on both halves of said property upon my death to reduce the capital gains, if sold during her life, or after her death. However, if Renee sells the Pasadena home prior to her death, then Mark's 50% separate community property interest shall pass to Maxine and she would be due 50% of the net proceeds from the sale.

2. *Although Renee shall have the benefit of Mark's half of the estate for the term of her life, (an estate for life), upon her death, Mark's 50% of the community property vested in the Pasadena home shall go to Maxine. Maxine shall have an equal say as to what is to happen with the house if it is to be sold. If Maxine is not alive, then the 50% goes to her issue, and should she be childless, then to whomever she names for this interest in the Pasadena home according to her own Revocable Trust, or Last Will and Testament;*
3. *Mark's interest in the house in Pismo Beach whereby Mark is to receive 50% interest in the sale of the house, or $250,000, plus 10% interest, (whichever is more), goes to Renee. Renee will have the right to collect the $250,000 plus interest, or 50% of the property value. Upon the sale of this Pismo property, the proceeds shall be used by*

Renee to pay off the mortgage on the Pasadena property. The Pismo condo shall be sold or refinanced to cover the cost of the mortgage by the year 2015. Failure to do this, for any reason, prior to February 1, 2015, will result in an immediate sell of the Pismo condo to benefit Renee's interest.

4. *All of the furniture and furnishings located at either the apartment in Carpinteria, or the house in Pasadena, with the exception of the personal gifts I leave to my daughter or others, goes to Renee.*
5. *The Jaguar and the Honda Fit go to Renee. I hope there is someone to give my 1979 "Flareside" pickup to before I die, but if not, it goes to Maxine.*
6. *I leave all my stocks and security investments, bank accounts, IRAs, and cash in a Bypass Trust with Renee as trustee for the benefit for her life, the remainder to Maxine. The details will be in the trust agreement which will also include an outright gift of a certain percent of this fund to go to Maxine upon my death as a reason for her to better her life immediately. This gift is explained below.*
7. *Etc.*

To Maxine:

1. *I give, devise and bequeath my 50% share of the rental home in Lompoc to Maxine. If Walter wants to buy Maxine out then the cost of the house will be determined by an appraiser chosen by Renee, an appraiser chosen/hired by Walt and if need be an appraiser chosen by both appraisers. This house will also go into the Bypass Trust and Renee will take a commission on its sale, if possible. The rest of the proceeds from the sale, up to 90% will go to pay down the mortgage on the apartments in Carpinteria. The remaining 10% to go to Maxine outright.*

2. *The fourplex in Carpinteria will be transferred into the name of Maxine at the appropriate time through our brokerage company, if not put in a QPRT first, but will be used for the benefit of Renee until Maxine reaches the age of 40 years old. At no time prior thereto will any further encumbrances be put upon the property. At the time of Maxine's fortieth birthday Renee will relinquish all rights and privileges to the condo and it will be owned by Maxine free and clear to aid in the benefit of Landsalot Realty, LLC. If Maxine is still living in San Francisco, and not using the condo as a personal residence, it shall remain under*

the management of Renee for the benefit of herself and the Landsalot Realty, LLC. If this arrangement is agreed to, Maxine shall share 50/50 on the net income, upon terms to which they both agree. At all times Maxine is the remainder beneficiary of the Bypass Trust and should anything happen to Renee at any time rendering her incapable of caring for the management of the condo, Maxine will be the successor trustee. But if Maxine chooses to sell the condo rather than live in it, Renee is entitled to 33 1/3% (thirty three and one-third per cent interest), or she can take full title to the house in Pasadena, whichever they agree upon. It is my strongest sentiment that this Carpinteria property shall pass to my daughter, a fifth generation Cornwall in Santa Barbara County, and that it remain the property of the Cornwall's legacy for as long as possible. Regardless of anything aforesaid, the property will pass to Maxine, no strings attached at the age of fifty."

The next thing this fictional Mark will do to break up the tough part, is to copy the list of everything he owns, or unlike George Washington, everything he can remember or cares about, and match them to the list of heirs. It could look something like this:

"Specific gifts by Mark Cornwall to persons other than his beloved Renee:

1. *Maxine gets my great aunt's chin and the remainder of any guns I have not specifically given away.*
2. *My watch goes to Maxine as well as the diamond necklace, particularly since her mother had it done.*
3. *The Cornwall family photos go to Maxine even though I don't think she appreciates the fact that her great-great grandfather had a grocery store on State Street in the 1920s and was taking photos from the yacht club flagship before there was even a breakwater in Santa Barbara. There is a plaque at the entrance honoring his assistance in getting the breakwater done.*
4. *The 1982 1,000 cc shovelhead Sportster is a tough one. Maybe I'll refurbish it and sell it too. If not, I'll give it to my friend, Bruce Jones. Maybe one of his boys wants it. Maybe Bruce wants it.*
5. *The Franklin Mint coins go to Maxine. Maybe the Bass brothers will try and corner the silver market again and silver will jump to $40.00 an once which was the price I accepted them for in 1979.*
6. *My copper sailing ship goes to Walt, another best friend. With it goes the first edition of The Pathfinder, and Cannery Row.*
7. *Etc.*

If Renee is to the first to die, she distributes her property as follows:

To Mark:"

This is where Mark repeats the process from above by listing all the specific gifts Renee will make if she is the first to die. Better yet would be for Renee to write out the text exactly the way she wants it.

A review of your estate plan is not complete unless you review all beneficiary designations of your life insurance, qualified/non-qualified plans, IRAs and other contractual arrangements. The above gifts pass by beneficiary designation in your Revocable Trust, rather than through probate or an insurance or pension trust. So do not forget about the beneficiaries you have previously named in your other contractual holdings to confirm that those beneficiaries are consistent with your overall estate planning goals.

CHAPTER TWENTY-SEVEN

Rethinking "Credit Shelter Trust"

After completing the above task you should pretty much feel like you are dead. After all, you have now given away everything you own. You have been forced into deciding who is going to get something and who is not. You realize it doesn't really matter because you can always change it, and you will probably outlive most of the people you just decided to give your stuff to if you died first. But on the other hand, you may never want to go through it again.

Now we are going to assume you live longer than the next two years and the marital tax exemption is $1 million per spouse in 2011. But this is a big assumption. As it stands in 2008 a spouse can put their $2 million marital tax exemption in the Bypass Trust. But what happens to this $2 million Bypass Trust when the tax exemption reverts back to $1 million?

Let's hope the $2 million exemption does not revert back to one million, just as it used to be. The tax will be at 55%, assuming no other legislation is passed. The problem is no one knows for sure, and Congress is not giving any hints other than what you have read here. As bad as this nation needs revenue during this recession of 2008, it would be naïve to think the "upper middle class" is going to get a tax break on their estate taxes.

We can only wish this will not affect the estate plans executed/completed prior to 2010. But if this is so, everyone should do their estate plan in 2010 when the marital tax exemption is unlimited. That is why everyone is hoping their extremely wealthy and very old uncle will be kind enough to expire in that year. Otherwise, you could put your entire estate in the Bypass Trust in 2010 and never worry about paying estate taxes again. It would not be added back into the Survivor's Trust when the survivor died, and the beneficiaries would pay no taxes on the earned income as it proceeded to compound in the trust year after year. It is difficult to imagine Congress would allow that to happen.

However, it does make you rethink the idea of a Qualified Personal Property Trust. Perhaps it is not just for the rich. Last year the median home price for a house in Santa Barbara, California was over $1 million. In ten years there is no reason the economy won't recycle, like it has twice in my lifetime in Santa Barbara, and then it will be worth $2 million. Wouldn't it be wonderful if that house was transferred to your children during your lifetime, and it was not added back into the value of your estate to be taxed?

As you recall from Chapter Eleven, the QPRT is the tool for the job and you can name your own term of years. You do not have to challenge outliving the IRS actuary table. In Mark Cornwall's case, if he wanted to leave the Carpinteria apartments to Maxine when she turns forty he would only have to live for eleven more years. He is now 58 years old. Can he make it to 69? The worse thing that can happen if he does not make it is that his family loses the deduction; or rather Maxine loses the deduction and would have to sell the condo to pay the taxes on it.

Hmmm? So far, Mark's chart looks like the one on the following page. But this is a rough draft. The exercise of going through it has forced Mark to rethink certain hurdles that must be crossed for the outcome to be equitable. The facts are, if he does not do something to transfer ownership before death, the fourplex presently valued at $1,495,200 may be worth twice that in ten tears. That would be $1,990,400 over the million dollar exemption presently waiting to be allocated in 2011.

Remember that this Economic Growth and Tax Relief Reconciliation Act was only enacted after the Democrats left office in 2000. The Republicans reformed the estate tax starting at $675,000 in 2001 and 55% tax on everything over that. In 1981 the maximum estate that could pass tax free was $600,000 But since President Bush has the worst approval rating of any president since keeping score, don't be surprised when you or your children have to sell the family home to pay for the new estate tax made into law by the new administration. Perhaps we will have to redo our estate plans to avoid the new estate tax laws in 2011.

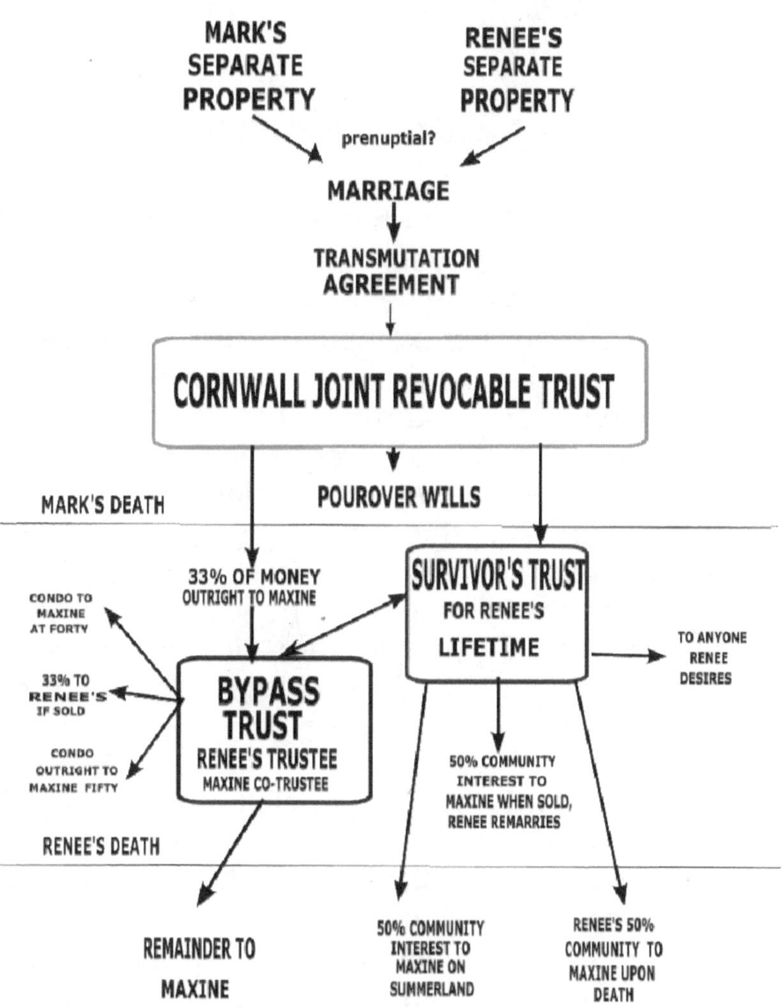
MARK'S SEPARATE PROPERTY
RENEE'S SEPARATE PROPERTY
prenuptial?
MARRIAGE
TRANSMUTATION AGREEMENT
CORNWALL JOINT REVOCABLE TRUST
POUROVER WILLS
MARK'S DEATH
33% OF MONEY OUTRIGHT TO MAXINE
SURVIVOR'S TRUST FOR RENEE'S LIFETIME
CONDO TO MAXINE AT FORTY
TO ANYONE RENEE DESIRES
33% TO RENEE'S IF SOLD
BYPASS TRUST
RENEE'S TRUSTEE
MAXINE CO-TRUSTEE
CONDO OUTRIGHT TO MAXINE FIFTY
50% COMMUNITY INTEREST TO MAXINE WHEN SOLD, RENEE REMARRIES
RENEE'S DEATH
REMAINDER TO MAXINE
50% COMMUNITY INTEREST TO MAXINE ON SUMMERLAND
RENEE'S 50% COMMUNITY TO MAXINE UPON DEATH

CHAPTER-TWENTY-EIGHT

The Need for Flexibility

Before deciding what the perfect finished product would be for your family's Joint Revocable Trust, it becomes evident from the chart you create that, as in the example of Mark Cornwall, it includes a provision for a transfer of property to his daughter Maxine through the Bypass Trust. Unfortunately, that trust is not the best choice to get the job done. What goes into the Bypass Trust is there for the benefit of the surviving spouse for her lifetime, and the remainder of the trust goes to the remainder beneficiary. But what if the surviving spouse (Renee) dies immediately after Mark? Then Maxine would have to deal with her father's in-laws.

That is why many couples use the QTIP Trust to make certain a child from a previous marriage will get her share upon the death of the surviving spouse. That is because although the survivor gets the benefits of any earnings from the QTIP Trust for life, she has no power of appointment over the assets. It is assured to go to the previous child regardless of the spendthrift habits of the surviving spouse. But if Mark's wife is extremely healthy and only eight years older than his daughter, it would cause Maxine to wait until the death of Renee before she would get the property.

The terms of the Bypass Trust could conceivably be so rock solid that there would be no question as to Renee giving up any interest she may have in the fourplex, and things would work out as planned as long as she is alive when Maxine turns forty to transfer the property. But if Renee is not living at the time of transfer to Maxine there could be room for one of Renee's heirs to take court action against the transfer, under some clever attorney's legal theory. However, a "no contest" clause may dissuade such actions. Regardless, it would ruin the entire plan.

The other problem Mark would be faced with if he used a QTIP Trust is that the value of the fourplex is added back into the surviving spouse's estate for tax purposes when she dies. So if Mark died tomorrow and he wanted to give his thirty year old daughter the 1.5 million dollar fourplex on her fortieth birthday, he could not do so if it was put in the QTIP Trust until Renee died, which is a disaster for two reasons:

1. Renee is 38 years old, only eight years older than Mark's daughter, so if Renee lived to be 100 years old, Mark's daughter would be 92 years old before she inherited the apartments—hardly the time to inherit start-up money.

2. Secondly, can you imagine the appreciation of the apartment's value

in 62 years, located on the last strip of beach front in Carpinteria before the estuary, let alone the house overlooking Pasadena from the hills above? Renee would have two beautiful houses valued in her estate that would end up being split, one house to the heirs, and one house for the government.

Therefore there are three alternate preferred ways to legitimately accomplish Mark's goal of wanting to transfer the fourplex to his daughter tax free, and to save tax dollars on his surviving wife's estate when she dies. These options are discussed below.

Bypass Trust v. QTIP

Because Mark owns the apartment fourplex separately as preserved in his Prenuptial Agreement, he could give this property to his daughter outright upon his death, but she would have to sell it because of estate taxes she could not pay. However, with the aid of the transmutation agreement Mark could give Renee 50% ownership in the fourplex, and both her half and Mark's half would go to his daughter, or her issue upon Maxine's fortieth birthday.

One way this could happen without using a QTIP Trust, (the QTIP being the safest way because there can be dramatic changes once the children have an ownership interest in the house and you are still alive), is by a firm agreement that is well stated in the terms and conditions of the Bypass Trust. Renee can promise to convey the property according to the terms above, and when the time comes she can do so. Mark has no reason to doubt her word. But if he died tomorrow, there is no reason to believe Renee would not remarry; Mark's own father remarried and was very happy the last ten years of his life. And unlike his father, Mark's grandfather, Mark's dad did not leave his entire estate to the new wife, as the majority of men do. That makes him a hero.

But years go by, and things change, and fortunately Mark's daughter is old enough to be the co-trustee of the Bypass Trust to work with Renee to make sure these agreements are kept.

But what if Maxine dies before Renee? There would be no certainty that Mark's 50% of community interest would pass on to Maxine's issue (child or children). Therefore, Mark had better use a QTIP Trust along with the Bypass Trust to make certain that in ten years nobody has forgotten the plan.

It is rumored amongst modern historians that Martha Washington took steps to interfere with her husband's prayer of emancipating their slaves. The situation was complicated because the slaves had intermarried and had children and grandchildren living at Mt. Vernon. Based on what she believed was her right of separate ownership of her slaves from her previous marriage, she sought out ways not to emancipate a certain number of slaves to keep in her estate. Whether the rumor is true or not, the point is, many things can change without you there to make it right.

QPRT

Given all these ifs, ands, ors and buts, which can crop up in a Bypass Transfer, the best credit shelter trust to use to leave the apartment complex for the benefit of Maxine may be the Qualified Personal Property Trust (QPRT). This allows Mark to create two QPRT trusts, one for himself and one for his wife, as separate grantors to Maxine. The grantee of each of these QPRTs will have a provision that Mark and Renee will live in the house for a term of ten years, after granting the condo to Maxine for her fortieth birthday, which will be in ten years. This way Mark and Renee use the condo as their own for a term of ten years, and even if Mark dies before that, thereby eliminating his estate tax deduction, his wife still gets a 50% gift deduction on the value of her estate for her gifting it to Maxine.

If Mark lives, they get a much larger deduction because of his age, and the $1.5 million fourplex, regardless of its appreciation, will not be added back into their estate. It transfers tax free to Maxine. This is because both Mark and Renee have a $1 million gift exemption each (or $2 million) to cover the additional $500,000, on the $1.5 million of the original price of the fourplex, assuming the marital tax exemption reverts to $1 million in 2011. If the exemption is $3.5 million, then there is no problem, and estate planning attorneys will be out of a lot of work.

The best part of the QPRT is the Cornwall's can still live in one of the apartments, as long as they pay a fair market rent, such as ¼ the mortgage payment. Mark doesn't think his one and only daughter will kick him out of the deluxe apartment after ten years for saving her more than a million dollars in taxes, which is what she would pay if he did nothing. However, what if she has suddenly come up with an ingenious product and marketing scheme and all she needs is the revenue from the sale of the fourplex to make it happen? Always remember a QPRT is irrevocable, meaning once you have done it, you can't take it back.

The reason I will not put an example of such a QPRT Trust in this book is because if you decided to use a QPRT for this purpose you definitely need professional assistance. You need a tax attorney to draw up the document to meet your needs, and you need sound tax advice from a CPA readily familiar with this type of trust. If you do not believe me go to www.irs.gov and search for "QPRT 2003-42 forms." That should be enough to send you to a tax expert to customize your trust, particularly if you want to turn it into a GRAT and receive a grantor's annuity, tax free, after the ten-year term. Tell them I sent you.

The FLP v. The LLC for Family Real Estate Transfers

Last week I went to the seminar of a nationally renowned legal scholar. He is on the board that writes the actual laws as they are worded when passed by the state legislature. It was his opinion, after forty years of estate administration, that the best vehicle to pass real property from parent to child is the Family Limited Partnership Trust (FLP). There is no doubt in my mind that paying this scholar $20,000 to complete that job would surpass the scrutiny of the IRS.

However, I respectfully disagree that the FLP is the proper choice, and base that decision on the advice of an IRS tax attorney who stated the IRS has an internal memo to investigate FLPs because of their 20-year history of abuse in failing to follow the letter of the law. As we discussed in Chapter Ten, a FLP is like waiving a red flag and daring the IRS to find a misuse, or controversial grey area which they can challenge under the law.

However, it could be a result of this closer IRS scrutiny that California passed its "Uniform Limited Partnership Act of 2008." The purpose of the act is clearly aimed at better defining the terms, conditions and limitations on how the FLP works, and what it should be used for as a form of family business entity. Whatever your situation, it is going to require some professional customization to make sure it is done correctly for your state.

In seems much wiser, in my opinion, to transfer the property and take the deduction using a Limited Liability Company for change of ownership in the family business. This would be particularly true if you had a family business with a legitimate business purpose.

You should know that a parent can transfer ownership of their real property to their children as long as the property is less than $1 million (in California) and there will be no tax on the transfer. But there are ramifications to the donor as far as the exemptions he or she can use when creating their estate plan.

One example of the need for crossing your Ts, if you are using an LLC for transfer purposes, you cannot transfer property into an LLC, then gift 50% of the partnership interest back to your daughter and expect an exemption from being reassessed by the County Appraiser. This type of gifting creates a new allocation of ownership, and is therefore reassessed. **The correct way is the parents should gift the property to the daughter, who may then contribute her interest into the LLC in exchange for a**

proportional percentage share of the partnership interest.

States may have different laws but federal regulations are the same everywhere. (Rev & Tax Code §63.1(c)(9) states that the real estate first be gifted to the child before it is contributed to the LLC.

Closing Statement

In case you have never seen a customized Revocable Trust to meet the needs of the type of family who has been drawn out for you in Chapter Twenty-Six, you must be aware that there are very expensive software programs on the market available to attorneys to help draw up these documents, and I have one.

The program will take the information I have provided and ask me questions to make certain I have covered every conceivable or foreseeable problem that may arise in the simple plan I have devised (or maybe not so simple). It ultimately formats a document that creates a Joint Revocable Trust, with a Survivor's Trust, a Bypass Trust and a QTIP Trust, with an option of a reverse QTIP disclaimer.

This particular program took my answers and wrote a 53 page document. It is so thick and full of boilerplate gobbledygook that I hate looking through it. To say it is thorough would be an understatement, but it is exactly the document

I would want if I was expecting trouble over my estate after I died.

Unless you are anticipating your Revocable Trust will end up in probate court, or will be scrutinized by the IRS, you may not need that many pages. For our purposes, we like to think neither of these events is going to happen. That is why we are doing a Revocable Trust - to stay out of probate court.

But the problem is neither you nor the attorney knows what is going to happen after you are gone. So much of what goes into the trust is in anticipation of something bad happening. What you may see as wasted paper may very well contain the provision that saves your estate from an IRS audit.

Afterall, who is going to be administrating this document? A Revocable Trust is intended to keep you out of probate court, but all this 53 page document does is prepare you for going to probate court, and at a considerable cost. If you are expecting non-cooperation from all family members and beneficiaries then you are better off going with a Last Will and Testament, as it will probably save your family attorney fees through court administration in the long run.

A Revocable Trust is a family affair, and as stated in the beginning of this book, that means you need someone you can trust to do what you want. That presupposes the beneficiaries have enough respect for your last desires that they will follow your wishes. You do not need a 53 page document to convey those wishes, or satisfy the legal requirements of the law. This 53 page document would mandate that the trustee seek out an attorney familiar with probate administration so they can tie up all the loose ends together. In many cases this is absolutely necessary, but usually not for the $3.5 to $7 million estate.

What you need is a document telling your trustee and your family exactly how you want to distribute your estate. There is no one else who ever needs to see your Revocable Trust. That is why it is private. But the courts are losing so much money over people avoiding probate that it will not be long before you are mandated to administrate the Revocable Trust only after paying a registration fee to the court.

Everything you put into your Revocable Trust does not have to be a boilerplate paragraph from a software program off the computer. As for specific gifts anybody could copy and recite the similar tangible gifts that were written informally above. But more likely than not, this text full of family or personal anecdotes would be delivered to the beneficiary of the gift, and not be put in the document draft itself, other than to identify the gift.

The only place you have to be specific to a "t" is when you are attempting to obtain tax benefits which affect the avoidance or deferment of taxes on earned income, capital gains, annuities, deferred income, charitable trust, or any other IRS tax implemented tool. You will need professional help to make sure every "i" is dotted.

Many things can happen without you there to make it right, but you can only do your best and enjoy it while you are here. In other words, spend your money the way you want.

You have the time to both spend and preserve your estate for posterity. It is a question of whether you are convinced how meaningful and helpful this Revocable Trust will be to the people who love you most, and whether you have the strength to give that love back to them before you go.

CONCLUSION

Think of George Washington lying on his death bed, Martha and close friends by his side. Then, just before he dies, he apologizes for never finishing his Last Will and Testament. It is difficult to imagine, is it not?

The reason for the difficulty is that George Washington is a symbol of utmost responsibility. That is part of his larger than life legacy, and one reason for the respect of our nation and his peers. He earned this respect leading a revolution by example. It still defines the man 209 years after his death. He has been the symbol of America's man who got the job done. He could have been King of America, but his vision of a democratic United States, dismissed that idea for reasons of pure ethics. It was not what he saw as fair for the generations to follow. He is a true hero, not a fictional power hero.

So which one are you? There are only two choices: hero, or the one who does not answer to his or her responsibility? I hope this book has helped you answer the challenge, and understand the chaos you are avoiding for your family, let alone the tax consequences, by attending to your estate plan now.

ACKNOWLEDGMENTS

I would like to acknowledge all of the attorneys of national and California acclaim, whose legal treatises and other scholarly writings and reviews, have contributed to this book in one way or the other. These expert's public and private opinions regarding very complicated issues, and their creative and humorous teachings on the subject of estate planning, have made this book possible.

More specifically, I would like to thank all contributors to the Continuing Education of the California Bar for their efforts to provide a forum to teach the most comprehensive and advanced information available to the general public through the education of the members of the bar.

I would also like to thank the Mt. Vernon Ladies Association of the Union for their support in keeping one of America's most beautiful monuments in first class condition with state-of-the-art museums and a live theatre. I would like to acknowledge Mr. James C. Rees and Mr. Stephan Signesi whose book, *George Washington's Leadership Lessons*, Wiley, 2007, was a motivating factor in writing this book.

Finally, I would like to thank the editors whose time, energy and thoughtfulness made this book a better read, more stylish and grammatically correct, and most importantly, of sound legal principles. I would like to thank Joanne Ando for her sharp eyes, Patricia Durham for her stylish etiquette, Henry Babcock for his computer know-how, Elizabeth Smith, Esq. for her legal mind, and Kathy Weber, for her final review. And, of course, I'd like to thank my loving wife D'Arcy, who helps me in every way.

APPENDIX

Instructions for the Estate Planning Questionnaire

At first blush, it may appear the following questionnaire is something more like a financial statement than a plan for putting your estate in order. But nothing questioned herein is going to be verified (yet), and secondly the idea is to start thinking about where your money is going to go after you die.

Death is never a happy subject, but it is going to happen to all of us. By answering these questions, you will review and consider all the pertinent issues necessary before putting your last wishes in writing.

It is also the very first piece of evidence showing your state of mind regarding your estate plan, in the event someone would ever make that an issue.

You may feel many of the questions intrude on your privacy. However, the point is for you to understand the nature of the personal relationship needed with your family and your attorney, so you can create the estate plan best suited for you.

The data you will be asked to provide includes:

1. Personal identity;
2. Your family ("natural objects of your bounty");
3. Your extended family as potential beneficiaries;
4. Potential trustees, guardians and conservators;
5. Assets, both separate and community;
6. Business interests;
7. Potential financial growth;
8. Liabilities;
9. Friends and relatives you trust most; and
10. Financial advisors.

Do the best you can. It is not a test. If nothing else, at least read through the questions and think about your answers.

Mark S. Cornwall
Attorney at Law

ESTATE PLANNING:

THE HEROES WAY FOR BABY BOOMERS

Estate Planning Questionnaire for Married Clients

1. It is important to know your full names:

   Birth certificate names ____________________
   ____

   Signature names ___________________________
   ____

   Common names _____________________________
   ____

2. Addresses:

   Residence(s) ______________________________
   ____

   Office(s) __________________________________
   ____

   Vacation Property(s) _______________________
   ____

P.O. Box ______________________________

____

3. Home phone, office phone, cell phone, facsimile, email addresses:

Husband: Best Phone # ______________
Email ______________________
Others _____________________

Wife: Best Phone # ______________
Email ______________________
Others _____________________

4. Dates and place of birth:

Husband ______________________________

Wife __________________________________

5. Citizenship:

Husband is a U.S. citizen? _______

Wife is a U.S. citizen? ___________

6. Marital History:

Date of Marriage: ____________________

Place of Marriage: ___________________

Date Husband and Wife came to _______ (state) if married elsewhere: __________

Children of this marriage (indicate if adopted):

Name Birth date

____

____

____

____

7. Husband's prior marriages:

Name of former wife(s) _______________

____

Year of termination of marriage(s) _____

____

Continuing legal obligations (alimony, child support) _______

Husband's children of prior marriage(s) (indicate if adopted):

Name Birth date
Residence

____

____

8. Wife's prior marriage(s):

Name of former husband(s) ___________

____

Year of termination of marriage(s) _____

____

Continuing legal obligations (alimony, child support) ___________________________

____

Wife's children of prior marriage(s) (indicate if adopted):

Name Birth date
Residence

____

____

____

____

9. Give the name of any adopting parent and which child:_______________________________

____

10. Deceased children and surviving descendents:

Name Surviving children

____

____

11. Grandchildren:

Name Parent Birth date

____

____

____

____

12. Name of parents (indicate whether living or deceased):

Husband's parents ____________________

____

Wife's parents ______________________

____

13. Are there any other relatives you are considering as beneficiaries of your estate such as sisters, brothers, nieces, nephews, etc?

Name	Birth Date	Relationship

14. Are there any friends or neighbors whom you are considering as beneficiaries of your estate?

____

____

15. Are there any specific gifts you are both sure you want to gift to specific people?

____

____

16. Are there any charities you are both sure you want to benefit from your estate?

____

____

17. Are there any persons named above you would consider for being the trustee of your estate?

____

____

18. Are there any persons named above you would consider for being the guardian of your children?

____

____

19. Occupation:
    Husband:
        Name of employer ____________
        ____
        Position or occupation _________
        ____
        Address ______________________
        ____
        Years on this job _____________
        Telephone ____________________
    Wife:
        Name of employer ____________
        ____
        Position or occupation _________
        ____
        Address ______________________
        ____
        Years on this job _____________
        Telephone ____________________

20. Social security numbers:

    Husband ___________________________
    Wife ______________________________

21. Income:

    Husband's annual earned income _______
    Wife's annual earned income ___________
    Other community property income ______
    Husband's annual separate property income ____________________
    Wife's annual separate property income ____________________

22. Assets:

This is an important part of your estate planning. A separate worksheet may be necessary. Husband and wife need to agree on what is separate property and what is community property. Much of this is decided by the form of title to the property.

ASSETS

Form of title	Current value
Real Property	________________
Cash and equivalents	________________
Securities	________________
Business interest	________________
Debts receivable	________________
Retirement benefits	________________
Death benefits	________________
Annuities	________________
Life insurance (face value)	________________
Art, jewelry, cars,	________________
Furniture, etc.	________________
Other assets	________________
	________________

What was your approximate net-worth the day before you were married?

Husband __________ Wife _________

Which of your holdings or assets do you believe have the most potential for significant appreciation in the future?

___

Do you anticipate obtaining assets of significant value in the future? If so, what is the plan?

___

If you own a business or partnership in a business, please explain your ownership interest and its value.

___

___

23. Major liabilities:

Mortgage(s):

1.______________________________

____

2.______________________________

____

3.______________________________

____

Commercial loan(s):

1.______________________________

____

2.______________________________

____

3.______________________________

____

Debts to private parties:

1.______________________________

____

2.______________________________

____

3.______________________________

____

Other debts (please describe):

1.______________________________

____

2.______________________________

____

3.______________________________

____

24. Have you guaranteed any loans?

Primary obligor   Amount guaranteed

____
____
____
____

25. Questions that affect the outcome of your estate:

Have you read this book or *Everything A Baby Boomer Should Know (Before Talking To An Attorney)?*
Yes _____ No _____

Have you entered into any prenuptial agreements or transmutation agreements affecting the ownership of your property?
Yes _____ No _____

Have you made any gifts over $10,000 after 1981?
Yes _____ No _____

Have you created any trust?
Yes _____ No _____

Have you received any substantial inheritance?
Yes _____ No _____

Do you expect to receive any substantial inheritance?
Yes _____ No _____

Are you the beneficiary of any trust?
Yes _____ No _____

Are there persons whom you may want to disinherit?
Yes _____ No _____

Are there any persons who have special needs you would like to provide for?
Yes _____ No _____

26. Please list your current advisors:

Accountant:______________________
____

Financial advisor:_________________
____

Life insurance agent:______________
____

Securities broker:________________
____

Investment advisor:_______________
____

Your most trusted friend:

Wife:______________________________
Husband:__________________________

Your most trusted relative:

Wife:______________________________
Husband:__________________________

27. Who is your first choice to be the conservator over your estate after your husband or wife dies?

Wife's first choice _________________
Husband's first choice _____________

Wife's second choice ______________
Husband's second choice __________

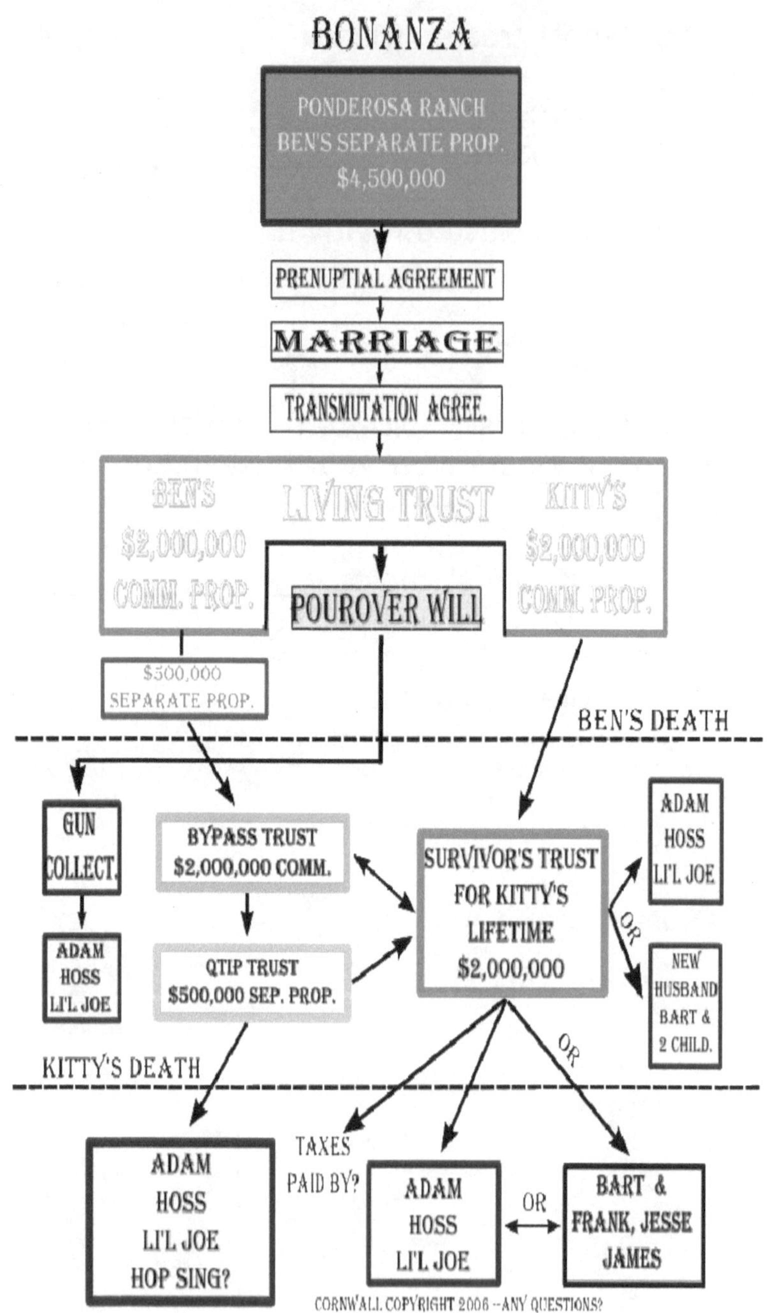
BONANZA
PONDEROSA RANCH
BEN'S SEPARATE PROP.
$4,500,000
PRENUPTIAL AGREEMENT
MARRIAGE
TRANSMUTATION AGREE.
BEN'S
$2,000,000
COMM. PROP.
LIVING TRUST
POUROVER WILL
KITTY'S
$2,000,000
COMM. PROP.
$500,000
SEPARATE PROP.
BEN'S DEATH
GUN
COLLECT.
ADAM
HOSS
LI'L JOE
BYPASS TRUST
$2,000,000 COMM.
QTIP TRUST
$500,000 SEP. PROP.
SURVIVOR'S TRUST
FOR KITTY'S
LIFETIME
$2,000,000
ADAM
HOSS
LI'L JOE
OR
NEW
HUSBAND
BART &
2 CHILD.
KITTY'S DEATH
OR
ADAM
HOSS
LI'L JOE
HOP SING?
TAXES
PAID BY?
ADAM
HOSS
LI'L JOE
OR
BART &
FRANK, JESSE
JAMES
CORNWALL COPYRIGHT 2006 --ANY QUESTIONS?

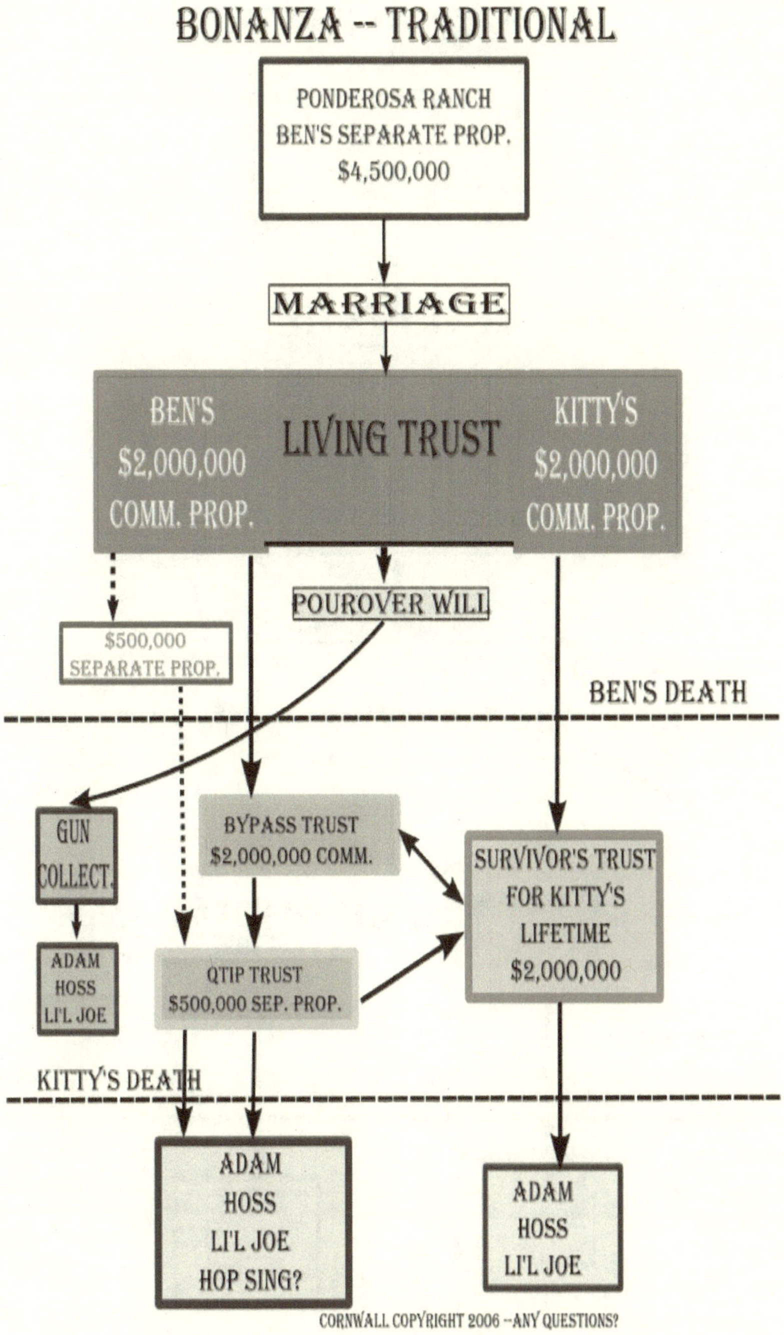
BONANZA -- TRADITIONAL
PONDEROSA RANCH
BEN'S SEPARATE PROP.
$4,500,000
MARRIAGE
BEN'S
$2,000,000
COMM. PROP.
LIVING TRUST
KITTY'S
$2,000,000
COMM. PROP.
POUROVER WILL
$500,000
SEPARATE PROP.
BEN'S DEATH
GUN
COLLECT.
BYPASS TRUST
$2,000,000 COMM.
SURVIVOR'S TRUST
FOR KITTY'S
LIFETIME
$2,000,000
ADAM
HOSS
LI'L JOE
QTIP TRUST
$500,000 SEP. PROP.
KITTY'S DEATH
ADAM
HOSS
LI'L JOE
HOP SING?
ADAM
HOSS
LI'L JOE
CORNWALL COPYRIGHT 2006 --ANY QUESTIONS?

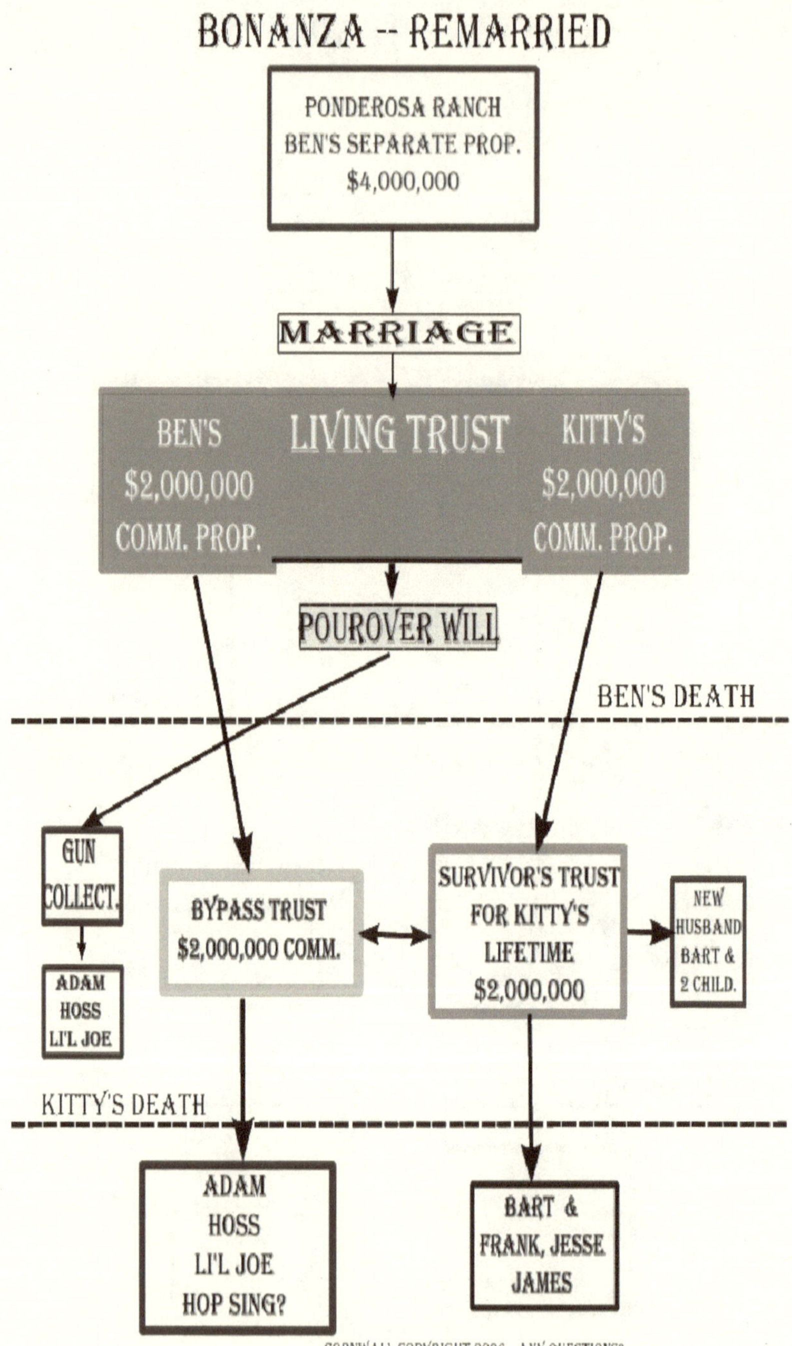
BONANZA -- REMARRIED
PONDEROSA RANCH
BEN'S SEPARATE PROP.
$4,000,000
MARRIAGE
BEN'S
$2,000,000
COMM. PROP.
LIVING TRUST
KITTY'S
$2,000,000
COMM. PROP.
POUROVER WILL
BEN'S DEATH
GUN
COLLECT.
ADAM
HOSS
LI'L JOE
BYPASS TRUST
$2,000,000 COMM.
SURVIVOR'S TRUST
FOR KITTY'S
LIFETIME
$2,000,000
NEW
HUSBAND
BART &
2 CHILD.
KITTY'S DEATH
ADAM
HOSS
LI'L JOE
HOP SING?
BART &
FRANK, JESSE
JAMES
CORNWALL COPYRIGHT 2006 -- ANY QUESTIONS?

Dr. Dentist And Nora

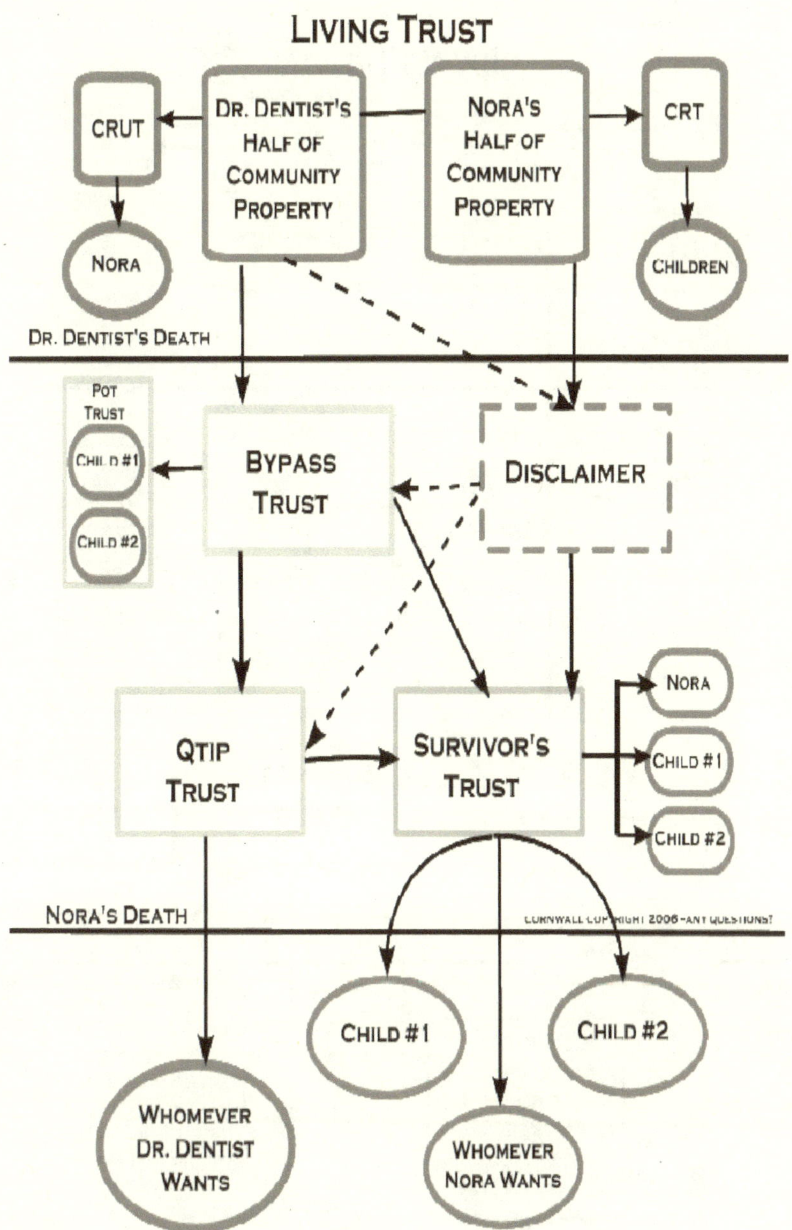

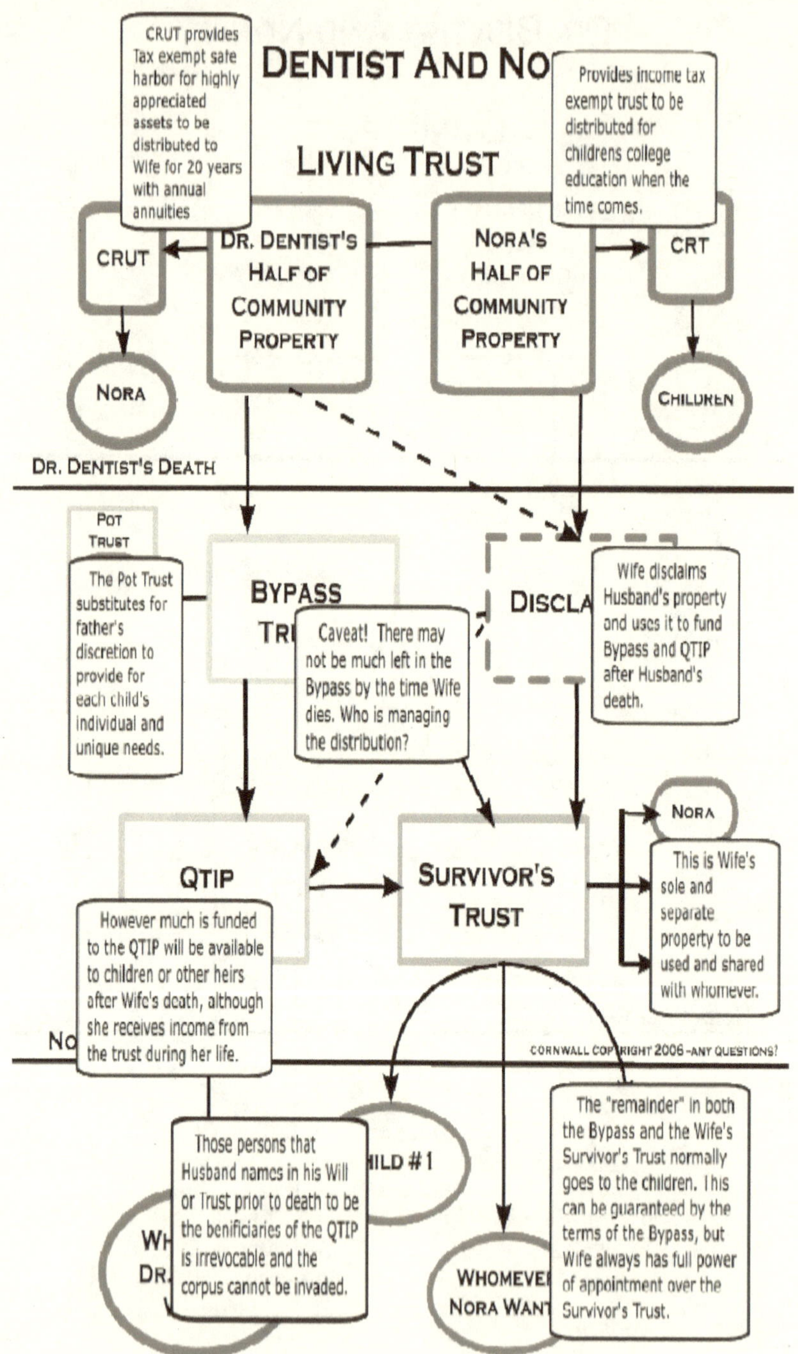
DENTIST AND NO
LIVING TRUST
CRUT provides Tax exempt safe harbor for highly appreciated assets to be distributed to Wife for 20 years with annual annuities
Provides income tax exempt trust to be distributed for childrens college education when the time comes.
CRUT
DR. DENTIST'S HALF OF COMMUNITY PROPERTY
NORA'S HALF OF COMMUNITY PROPERTY
CRT
NORA
CHILDREN
DR. DENTIST'S DEATH
POT TRUST
The Pot Trust substitutes for father's discretion to provide for each child's individual and unique needs.
BYPASS
TR
Caveat! There may not be much left in the Bypass by the time Wife dies. Who is managing the distribution?
DISCLA
Wife disclaims Husband's property and uses it to fund Bypass and QTIP after Husband's death.
QTIP
SURVIVOR'S TRUST
NORA
This is Wife's sole and separate property to be used and shared with whomever.
However much is funded to the QTIP will be available to children or other heirs after Wife's death, although she receives income from the trust during her life.
NO
CORNWALL COP RIGHT 2006 -ANY QUESTIONS?
Those persons that Husband names in his Will or Trust prior to death to be the benificiaries of the QTIP is irrevocable and the corpus cannot be invaded.
HILD #1
WH
DR.
WHOMEVE
NORA WAN
The "remainder" in both the Bypass and the Wife's Survivor's Trust normally goes to the children. This can be guaranteed by the terms of the Bypass, but Wife always has full power of appointment over the Survivor's Trust.

WALT THE PLUMBING CONTRACTOR

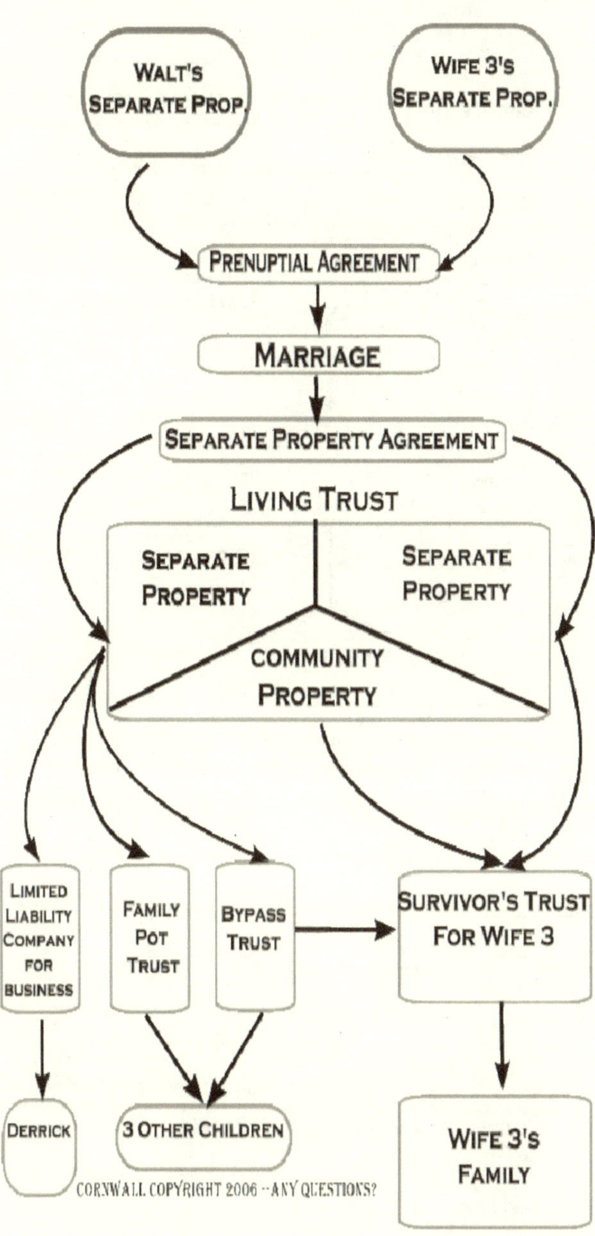

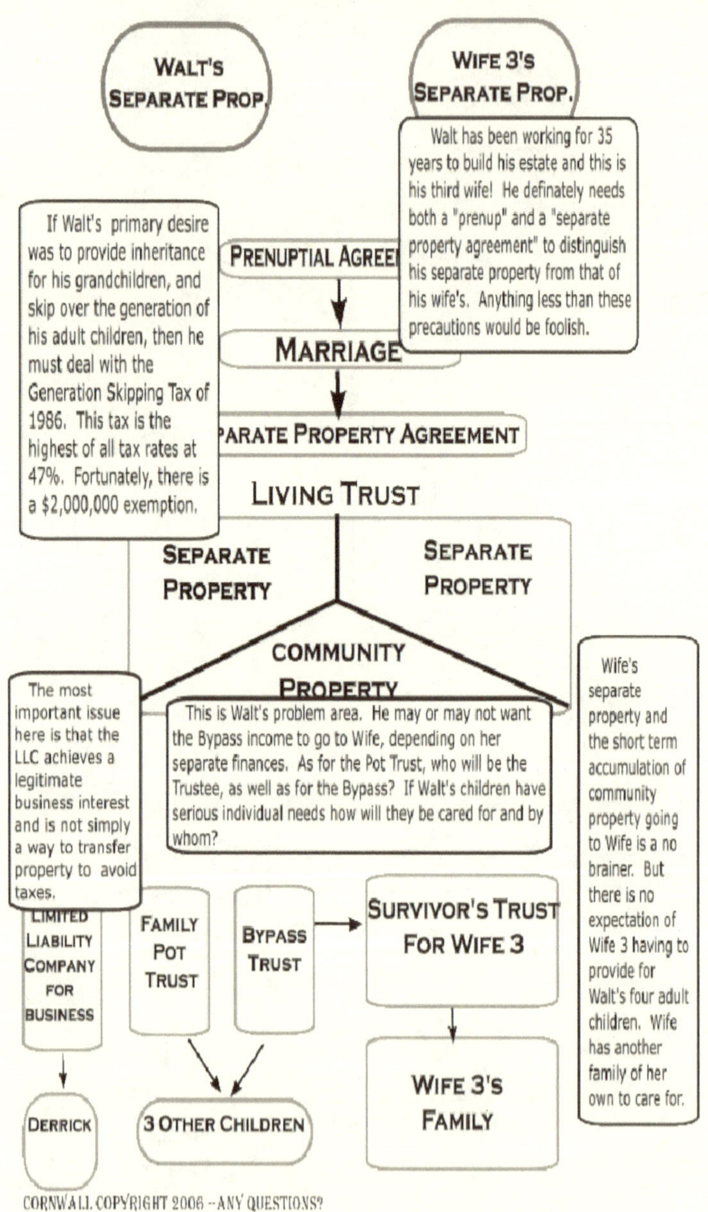
WALT THE PLUMBING CONTRACTOR
WALT'S SEPARATE PROP.
WIFE 3'S SEPARATE PROP.
Walt has been working for 35 years to build his estate and this is his third wife! He definately needs both a "prenup" and a "separate property agreement" to distinguish his separate property from that of his wife's. Anything less than these precautions would be foolish.
If Walt's primary desire was to provide inheritance for his grandchildren, and skip over the generation of his adult children, then he must deal with the Generation Skipping Tax of 1986. This tax is the highest of all tax rates at 47%. Fortunately, there is a $2,000,000 exemption.
PRENUPTIAL AGREE
MARRIAGE
ARATE PROPERTY AGREEMENT
LIVING TRUST
SEPARATE PROPERTY
SEPARATE PROPERTY
COMMUNITY PROPERTY
The most important issue here is that the LLC achieves a legitimate business interest and is not simply a way to transfer property to avoid taxes.
This is Walt's problem area. He may or may not want the Bypass income to go to Wife, depending on her separate finances. As for the Pot Trust, who will be the Trustee, as well as for the Bypass? If Walt's children have serious individual needs how will they be cared for and by whom?
Wife's separate property and the short term accumulation of community property going to Wife is a no brainer. But there is no expectation of Wife 3 having to provide for Walt's four adult children. Wife has another family of her own to care for.
LIMITED LIABILITY COMPANY FOR BUSINESS
FAMILY POT TRUST
BYPASS TRUST
SURVIVOR'S TRUST FOR WIFE 3
DERRICK
3 OTHER CHILDREN
WIFE 3'S FAMILY
CORNWALL COPYRIGHT 2006 --ANY QUESTIONS?

Start Your Own Chart

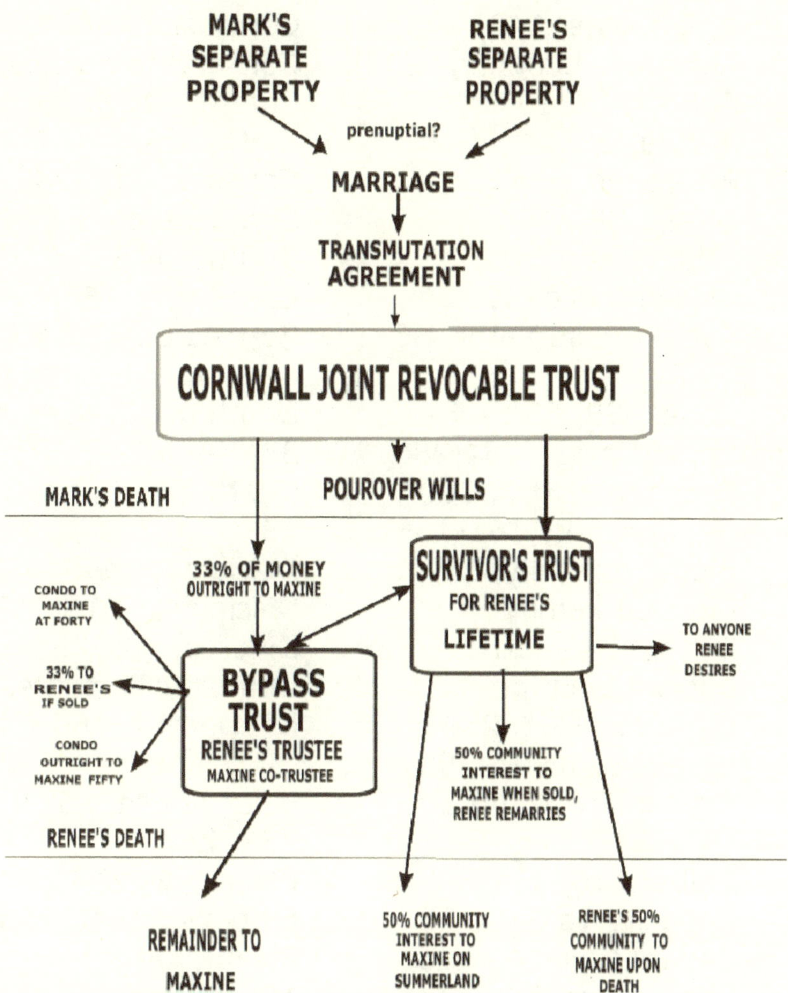

Index

www.ingramcontent.com/pod-product-compliance
Lightning Source LLC
LaVergne TN
LVHW050928080826
845145LV00001B/247